A Hundred White Daffodils

OTHER BOOKS BY JANE KENYON

From Room to Room
Twenty Poems of Anna Akhmatova (Translations)
The Boat of Quiet Hours
Let Evening Come
Constance
Otherwise: New & Selected Poems

A
Hundred

White
Daffodils

———

Jane

Kenyon

ESSAYS, THE AKHMATOVA TRANSLATIONS,
NEWSPAPER COLUMNS, NOTES, INTERVIEWS,
AND ONE POEM

Graywolf Press
Saint Paul, Minnesota

Publication of this volume is made possible in part by a grant provided by the Minnesota State Arts Board through an appropriation by the Minnesota State Legislature, and by a grant from the National Endowment for the Arts. Significant support has also been provided by Dayton's, Mervyn's, and Target stores through the Dayton Hudson Foundation, the Bush Foundation, the McKnight Foundation, the General Mills Foundation, the St. Paul Companies, and other generous contributions from foundations, corporations, and individuals. To these organizations and individuals we offer our heartfelt thanks.

Published by Graywolf Press
2402 University Avenue, Suite 203
Saint Paul, Minnesota 55114
All rights reserved.

www.graywolfpress.org

Published in the United States of America

ISBN 1-55597-291-8

2   4   6   8   9   7   5   3   1
First Graywolf Printing, 1999

Library of Congress Catalog Card Number: 99-60732

Cover design: Tree Swenson, Sarah Purdy
Cover photograph: William Abranowicz
Digital artwork: Nina M. Douglas

Acknowledgments

Grateful acknowledgment is made to the editors of the following in which the material listed below first appeared:

Twenty Poems of Anna Akhmatova, translated from the Russian by Jane Kenyon with Vera Sandomirsky Dunham, Eighties Press/Ally Press, 1985

"'Good-by and Keep Cold,'" *Yankee,* November 1990

"The Moment of Peonies," *Yankee,* June 1991

"Notes of a Novice Hiker," as "Above the Tree Line," *Yankee,* April 1999

"Edna Powers," *The Concord Monitor,* 3 May 1989

"Estonia and New Hampshire," *The Concord Monitor,* 8 June 1989

"The Mailbox," *The Concord Monitor,* 29 July 1989

"Season of Change and Loss," *The Concord Monitor,* 28 October 1989

"Every Year the Light," *The Concord Monitor,* 7 December 1989

"The Five-and-Dime," *The Concord Monitor,* 31 January 1990

"A Gardener of the True Vine," *The Concord Monitor,* 31 March 1990

"Summer Comes Alive," *The Concord Monitor,* 25 June 1990

"The Physics of Long Sticks," *The Concord Monitor,* 4 September 1990

"The Honey Wagon," *The Concord Monitor,* 27 April 1991

"Bulbs Planted in the Fall," *The Concord Monitor,* 28 June 1991

"A Day to Loaf," *The Concord Monitor,* 30 August 1991

"A Garden of My Dreams," *The Concord Monitor,* 28 January 1992

"The Mud Will Dry," *The Concord Monitor,* 18 April 1992

"The Shadows," *The Concord Monitor,* 6 July 1992

"Dreams of Math," *The Concord Monitor,* 12 September 1992

"Snakes in This Grass?" *The Concord Monitor,* 16 March 1993

"Reflections on a Roadside Warning," *The Concord Monitor,* 16 June 1993

"Poetry and the Mail," *The Concord Monitor,* 16 August 1993

"Kicking the Eggs," *Walking Swiftly: Writings & Images on the Occasion of Robert Bly's 65th Birthday,* edited by Thomas R. Smith, Nineties Press/Ally Press, 1992

"A Proposal for New Hampshire Writers" and "Thoughts on the Gifts of Art," *Ex Libris,* New Hampshire State Council on the Arts, 1992

"Notes for a Lecture: 'Everything I Know About Writing Poetry,'" *The Writer's Chronicle,* March/April 1999

"An Interview with Bill Moyers," *The Language of Life: A Festival of Poets,* edited by Bill Moyers, Doubleday, 1995

"An Interview with David Bradt," *The Plum Review,* 1996

"An Interview with Marian Blue," *AWP Chronicle,* May/Summer 1995

"Woman, Why Are You Weeping?" *The Atlantic Monthly,* April 1999

Contents

IV

Notes on Literature and the Arts

V

Interviews

VI

A Poem

Introduction

When Jane collected her poems for *Otherwise,* she did not speak of a
book like this one, that would assemble her translations, interviews,
and miscellaneous prose. But a year or two before she took sick, Jane
started to think about a prose book gathered from the columns she
wrote for the *Concord Monitor,* our local daily paper. She showed a
preliminary group of columns to Scott Walker, then her editor at
Graywolf, and made some changes in the pieces as published. She had
written and published a few essays elsewhere; before she became ill,
she was working on others. If she had lived, Jane would have written
more prose.

Her translations from Akhmatova are the earliest work here. Ally
Press published Jane's *Twenty Poems of Anna Akhmatova* in 1985, with
the Russian *en face.* Her introduction records her gratitude to Robert
Bly for setting her this task, gratitude that she expands upon later in
this book—in her essay on Bly, and in an interview. Her introduction
describes her collaboration with Vera Sandomirsky Dunham, who
supplied the language and who contributed to Jane's love for the great
Russian poet. Vera Sandomirsky came to the United States from
Russia in 1940. Scholar and critic, she taught at Columbia, at Wayne
State in Detroit, and at Stony Brook on Long Island. She worked on
translations from the Russian with other American poets: Robert Bly,
Louis Simpson, William Jay Smith. Retired now, she lives outside
Boston.

Jane felt that her five years of obsessive attention to Akhmatova
contributed immensely to her work. I remember her showing me a
poem printed in her first book, "Full Moon in Winter," anxious that

it might owe so much to Akhmatova that it amounted to plagiarism. It doesn't, but as she worked with Akhmatova's early lyrics, condensations of strong feeling into compact images both visual and aural, she practiced making the kind of poetry she admired most—an art that embodied powerful emotion by means of the luminous particular. Her introduction to the translations is her only essay in literary criticism. It is a pity that she never wrote about John Keats, Anton Chekhov, Elizabeth Bishop, or Geoffrey Hill, all of whom she greatly admired and learned from.

The second section assembles a miscellany of essays beginning with two garden pieces Jane wrote for the end page of *Yankee*. She wrote other pieces on gardening, heretofore uncollected, and an account of her first ascent of Mount Washington. She climbed it three times in all, last in 1993 not long before her illness. One of her newspaper columns described her second climb, a column omitted from this book because "Notes of a Novice Hiker" treats similar material more fully.

Her memoir of religion in childhood remains unfinished, and I title it with its first words. When she worked on this memoir in 1992, she ended by announcing an extraordinary experience—and became speechless when she tried to name it. I believe that this experience occurred in 1980. I came home after three or four days away and found Jane in a quiet, exalted, shining mood. She told me that something extraordinary had happened while I was away. She had felt a presence with her in the room that lingered with her. She associated it with the Holy Spirit, and it seemed to her female. This experience entered her poems, as it entered her soul and remained there except in times of depression. I think of "Briefly It Enters and Briefly Speaks" and "Who." Note also the essay that ends this section, "Gabriel's Truth."

The third section here comprises columns Jane wrote for the *Concord Monitor*. For years I had cajoled Jane about writing prose. She took on these columns because she could address her neighbors, and because she thought she might learn how to write in paragraphs. I asked the editor what he remembered of Jane's recruitment to the *Monitor*'s Forum—a feature in which a revolving group of writers each contributes a few columns a year. Mike Pride wrote me that when he asked Jane to write an occasional column "she was a little reluctant," but that she came to enjoy her relationship with the *Monitor*'s readers. "I asked Jane after the Wilmot Town Hall reading in January 1993 [for Bill Moyers's 'A Life Together'] to write a piece about manic depression. She wrote me: 'I do want to see a piece in the *Monitor* on manic-depression, but all the excitement of the filming has pulled me pretty far off center. I need to get my concentration back.'" She never did that column, and wrote her last in December of 1993, a month before diagnosis. Mike did not know the extent of her debility, and "In April 1994, to my invitation to continue, she wrote: 'I find myself so disabled by the treatment that I really can't be sure of my ability to write anything. You're the person who got me writing prose, and I'm always grateful for it.'"

Because she was scrupulous about deadlines, Jane wrote columns on occasion when she was too depressed to write a column. She knew that the work was uneven. I found a piece of paper with her collection of columns, notes for revision or exclusion: "Gulf War" is "dated." "Estonian—rework or cut, putting it in time" [she meant historical context]. In all I have omitted four of her columns, remembering Jane's dissatisfactions, consulting with her closest friends.

In the fourth section of this book I collect some further words on literature and the arts. I include notes for a talk (published in *AWP Chronicle*, 1999) that she gave at a summer workshop in 1991—she called it "Everything I Know About Writing Poetry"—which provide a telegraphic summary of Jane's poetic commandments.

The fifth part of *A Hundred White Daffodils* is three interviews, all from 1993. The Bill Moyers interview is abstracted from a conversation on camera that took two hours on 30 January 1993.

David Bradt is a friend who teaches at New Hampshire College. The Marian Blue interview took place over a long breakfast in Norfolk, Virginia, that April, where the Associated Writing Programs had its annual meeting. We altered the transcript of the Blue interview in Seattle, at the time of Jane's bone marrow transplant, when she was too sick to read or write. I read her sentences aloud, and we made small changes. (I remember that we omitted the word "Well," from the beginnings of her sentences.) I have shortened this interview, mainly by cutting wordy paragraphs of my own.

This book ends with a poem, "Woman, Why Are You Weeping?" omitted from *Otherwise* but worthy of a place there. Jane worked hard on this poem in 1992, after our first trip to India. At some point that year she set it aside, to return to later. When she asked me to fetch her new and uncollected poems from her study, 12 April 1995, this poem was not in the group. In our hurry to assemble *Otherwise* while she was able, I suggested that we might include "Woman, Why Are You Weeping?" Her negative was firm, and I was in no mood to argue with her. I wonder: If I had found a copy, and read it aloud to her, would she have included it? I don't know, but I feel that this poem of spiritual loss includes some of Jane's best Christian writing, as well as brilliant images from India, a country she loved. My editorial helpers for this collection—thanks to Gregory Orr, Joyce Peseroff, and Alice Mattison—agree that this poem belongs in print.

Donald Hall, 1998

I

Twenty Poems of
Anna Akhmatova

❧

Translated from the Russian with
Vera Sandomirsky Dunham

Introduction (1984)

As we remember Keats for the beauty and intensity of his shorter poems, especially the odes and sonnets, so we revere Akhmatova for her early lyrics—brief, perfectly made verses of passion and feeling. Images build emotional pressure:

> And sweeter even than the singing of songs
> is this dream, now becoming real:
> the swaying of branches brushed aside
> and the faint ringing of your spurs.

I love the sudden twists these poems take, often in the last line. In one poem the recollection of a literary party ends with the first frank exchange of glances between lovers. Another poem lists sweet-smelling things—mignonette, violets, apples—and ends, astonishingly, ". . . we have found out forever/that blood smells only of blood." These poems celebrate the sensual life, and Akhmatova's devoted attention to details of sense always serves feeling:

> With the hissing of a snake the scythe cuts down
> the stalks, one pressed hard against another.

The snake's hissing is accurate to the sound of scythe mowing, and more than accurate: by using the snake for her auditory image, Akhmatova compares this rural place, where love has gone awry, to the lost Eden.

Akhmatova was born Anna Gorenko near Odessa in 1889. Soon her family moved to Tsarskoe Selo, near St. Petersburg, and there she

3

began her education. Studying French, she learned to love Baudelaire and Verlaine. At the age of ten she became seriously ill, with a disease never diagnosed, and went deaf for a brief time. As she recovered she wrote her first poems.

Money was not abundant in the Gorenko household, nor was tranquility. Akhmatova did not get on with her father, Andrei Gorenko, a naval engineer who lectured at the Naval Academy in St. Petersburg—also a notorious philanderer whose money went to his mistresses. (We know little of Akhmatova's relationship with her mother.) Akhmatova's brother Victor recalls an occasion when the young girl asked their father for money for a new coat. When he refused she threw off her clothes and became hysterical. (See *Akhmatova: Poems, Correspondence, Reminiscences, Iconography:* Ardis.) Andrei Gorenko deserted his family in 1905. A few years later, hearing that his daughter wrote verse, he asked her to choose a pen name. He wished to avoid the ignominy, as he put it, of "a decadent poetess" in the family. She took her Tartar great-grandmother's name.

When Akhmatova was still a schoolgirl she met Nikolai Gumilev, a poet and founder of Acmeism who became her mentor and her first husband. Nadezhda Mandelstam has said that Akhmatova rarely spoke of her childhood; she seemed to consider her marriage to Gumilev the beginning of her life. (See Mandelstam's *Hope Abandoned:* Atheneum.) She was slow to accept his proposal. He sought her attention by repeated attempts at suicide until she finally married him in 1910. The bride's family did not attend the ceremony. Having won her at last, Gumilev promptly left to spend six months in Africa. On his return, while still at the train station, he asked her if she had been writing. By reply she handed him the manuscript of *Evening,* her first book.

Their son, Lev Gumilev, was born in 1912, the same year Akhmatova published *Evening.* By 1917, when she was twenty-eight, she had brought out two more books, *Rosary* and *White Flock.* Despite the historical tumult of World War I and the Revolution, her poetry quickly became popular. But tumult was private as well as public: by 1918 her marriage had failed; Akhmatova divorced Gumilev and the same autumn married the Assyriologist V. K. Shileiko. This unhappy alliance—Shileiko burned his wife's poems in the samovar—lasted for six years. (See Amanda Haight's biography, *Akhmatova: A Poetic Pilgrimage:* Oxford.) Ordinary family life eluded Akhmatova, who went through many love affairs. Before her divorce from Shileiko, she lived in a ménage à trois with Nikolai Punin and his wife; Punin later became her third husband. Motherhood was not easy. ("The lot of a mother is a bright torture: I was not worthy of it. . . .") For the most part, Gumilev's mother raised her grandson Lev.

In the years following her early triumphs Akhmatova suffered many torments, as the Soviet regime hardened into tyranny. Gumilev was executed in 1921 for alleged anti-Bolshevik activity. Early in the twenties Soviet critics denounced Akhmatova's work as anachronistic and useless to the Revolution. The Central Committee of the Communist Party forbade publication of her verse; from 1923 to 1940, none of her poetry appeared in print. The great poems of her maturity, *Requiem,* and *Song Without a Hero,* exist in Russia today only by underground publication, or *samizdat.*

During the Stalinist terror of the 1930s the poet's son Lev and her husband Punin were imprisoned. Akhmatova's fellow Acmeist and close friend Osip Mandelstam died in a prison camp in 1938. (Punin died in another camp fifteen years later.) During the Second World War the Committee of the Communist Party of Leningrad evacuated Akhmatova to Tashkent in Uzbekistan. There she lived in a small, hot room, in ill health, with Osip Mandelstam's widow Nadezhda.

In 1944 Akhmatova returned to Leningrad, to a still-higher wave of official antagonism. In a prominent literary magazine, Andrei Zhdanov denounced her as ". . . a frantic little fine lady flitting between the boudoir and the chapel . . . half-nun, half-harlot." The

Union of Soviet Writers expelled her. A new book of poems, already in print, was seized and destroyed. For many years she supported herself only by working as a translator from Asiatic languages and from French, an activity she compared to "eating one's own brain" (Haight).

The final decade of her life was relatively tranquil. During the thaw that followed Stalin's death, the government released Lev Gumilev from labor camp and reinstated Akhmatova in the Writer's Union. She was permitted to publish and to travel. In Italy and England she received honors and saw old friends. She died in March 1966, and was buried at Komarovo, near Leningrad.

Akhmatova's work ranges from the highly personal early lyrics through the longer, more public and political *Requiem,* on to the allusive and cryptic *Poem Without a Hero.* The early poems embody Acmeist principles. Acmeism grew out of the Poet's Guild, which Nikolai Gumilev and Sergei Gorodetsky founded in 1912—fifteen poets who met regularly to read poems and argue aesthetic theory. At one meeting, Gumilev proposed an attack on Symbolism with its "obligatory mysticism." He proposed Acmeism as an alternative; Acmeism held that a rose is beautiful in itself, not because it stands for something. These poets announced that they were craftsmen not priests, and dedicated themselves to clarity, concision, and perfection of form. They summed up their goals in two words: "beautiful clarity." Gumilev himself, Akhmatova, and Osip Mandelstam were the leading Acmeists, and the movement thrived for a decade.

Written so many years later, *Requiem* and *Poem Without a Hero* naturally moved past Akhmatova's early poems in intention and in scope. They are manifestly political and historical. *Requiem* records the terror of the purges in the 1930s, commemorating the women who stood waiting outside prison gates with parcels for husbands, sons, and brothers; Akhmatova compares the suffering of these women to Mary's at the Crucifixion. In the prefatory note to *Poem Without a Hero* Akhmatova says: "I dedicate this poem to its first listeners—my friends and countrymen who perished in Leningrad during the siege."

These translations are free-verse versions of rhymed and metered poems. Losing the formal perfection of the Russian verses—much of the "beautiful clarity"—has been a constant source of frustration and sadness to me and to my co-worker, Vera Sandomirsky Dunham. But something, I think, crosses the barrier between our languages. Because it is impossible to translate with fidelity to form *and* to image, I have sacrificed form for image. Image embodies feeling, and this embodiment is perhaps the greatest treasure of lyric poetry. In translating, I mean to place the integrity of the image over all other considerations.

Translation provides many frustrations. It seems impossible to translate a single Russian syllable that means "What did he have to do that for?" Trying to translate lines about a native place—so important to Akhmatova, who firmly refused expatriation—how does one render *rodnoi*, which means "all that is dear to me, familiar, my own . . ."? I remember Vera clapping her hands to her head and moaning, "This will sink us . . ."

There are times when—in the interest of cadence, tone, or clarity—I have altered punctuation or moved something from one line to another. Often I needed to shift the verb from the end to the beginning of the sentence. Sometimes a word, translated from Russian as the dictionary would have it, made impossible English. I list significant variations from the original in notes at the back of this book. We have translated from the two volume *Works,* edited by G. P. Struve and B. A. Filippov, published by Interlanguage Literary Associates in 1965.

I want to thank Robert Bly, who first encouraged me to read Akhmatova, and later to translate these poems. I also thank Lou Teel, who, as a student of Russian at Dartmouth, helped me begin the work. I owe special thanks to Vera Sandomirsky Dunham, a busy scholar, teacher, and lifelong lover of these poems. Her fear that a free-verse translation of Akhmatova is fundamentally misconceived has not prevented her from offering her time, her erudition, and her hospitality.

J. K.

Poems from

Evening (1912)
Rosary (1914)
White Flock (1917)

❧

1

The memory of sun weakens in my heart,
grass turns yellow,
wind blows the early flakes of snow
lightly, lightly.

Already the narrow canals have stopped flowing;
water freezes.
Nothing will ever happen here—
not ever!

Against the empty sky the willow opens
a transparent fan.
Maybe it's a good thing I'm not
your wife.

The memory of sun weakens in my heart.
What's this? Darkness?
It's possible. And this may be the first night
of winter.

1911

2

Evening hours at the desk.
And a page irreparably white.
The mimosa calls up the heat of Nice,
a large bird flies in a beam of moonlight.

And having braided my hair carefully for the night
as if tomorrow braids will be necessary,
I look out the window, no longer sad, —
at the sea, the sandy slopes.

What power a man has
who doesn't ask for tenderness!
I cannot lift my tired eyes
when he speaks my name.

1913

3

I know, I know the skis
will begin again their dry creaking.
In the dark blue sky the moon is red,
and the meadow slopes so sweetly.

The windows of the palace burn
remote and still.
No path, no lane,
only the iceholes are dark.

Willow, tree of nymphs,
don't get in my way.
Shelter the black grackles, black
grackles among your snowy branches.

1913

4
The Guest

Everything's just as it was: fine hard snow
beats against the dining room windows,
and I myself have not changed:
even so, a man came to call.

I asked him: "What do you want?"
He said, "To be with you in hell."
I laughed: "It seems you see
plenty of trouble ahead for us both."

But lifting his dry hand
he lightly touched the flowers.
"Tell me how they kiss you,
tell me how you kiss."

And his half-closed eyes
remained on my ring.
Not even the smallest muscle moved
in his serenely angry face.

Oh, I know it fills him with joy—
this hard and passionate certainty
that there is nothing he needs,
and nothing I can keep from him.

1 January 1914

5

N.V.N.

There is a sacred, secret line in loving
which attraction and even passion cannot cross,—
even if lips draw near in awful silence
and love tears at the heart.

Friendship is weak and useless here,
and years of happiness, exalted and full of fire,
because the soul is free and does not know
the slow luxuries of sensual life.

Those who try to come near it are insane
and those who reach it are shaken by grief.
So now you know exactly why
my heart beats no faster under your hand.

1915

6

Like a white stone in a deep well
one memory lies inside me.
I cannot and will not fight against it:
it is joy and it is pain.

It seems to me that anyone who looks
into my eyes will notice it immediately,
becoming sadder and more pensive
than someone listening to a melancholy tale.

I remember how the gods turned people
into things, not killing their consciousness.
And now, to keep these glorious sorrows alive,
you have turned into my memory of you.

1916
Slepnevo

7

Everything promised him to me:
the fading amber edge of the sky,
and the sweet dreams of Christmas,
and the wind at Easter, loud with bells,

and the red shoots of the grapevine,
and waterfalls in the park,
and two large dragonflies
on the rusty iron fencepost.

And I could only believe
that he would be mine
as I walked along the high slopes,
the path of burning stones.

1916

Poems from

Plantain (1921)

8

Yes I loved them, those gatherings late at night,—
the small table, glasses with frosted sides,
fragrant vapor rising from black coffee,
the fireplace, red with powerful winter heat,
the biting gaiety of a literary joke,
and the first helpless and frightening glance of my love.

1917

9

Twenty-first. Night. Monday.
Silhouette of the capitol in darkness.
Some good-for-nothing—who knows why—
made up the tale that love exists on earth.

People believe it, maybe from laziness
or boredom, and live accordingly:
they wait eagerly for meetings, fear parting,
and when they sing, they sing about love.

But the secret reveals itself to some,
and on them silence settles down . . .
I found this out by accident
and now it seems I'm sick all the time.

1917

10

There is a certain hour every day
so troubled and heavy . . .
I speak to melancholy in a loud voice
not bothering to open my sleepy eyes.
And it pulses like blood,
is warm like a sigh,
like happy love
is smart and nasty.

1917

11

We walk along the hard crest of the snowdrift
toward my white, mysterious house,
both of us so quiet,
keeping the silence as we go along.
And sweeter even than the singing of songs
is this dream, now becoming real:
the swaying of branches brushed aside
and the faint ringing of your spurs.

January 1917

12

All day the crowd rushes one way, then another;
its own gasping frightens it still more,
and laughing skulls fly on funereal banners,
prophesying from the river's far side.
For this I sang and dreamed!
They have torn my heart in two.
How quiet it is after the volley!
Death sends patrols into every courtyard.

1917

13

The river flows without hurry through the valley,
a house with many windows rises on the hill—
and we live as people did under Catherine;
hold church services at home, wait for harvest.
Two days have passed, two days' separation;
a guest comes riding along a golden wheatfield.
In the parlor he kisses my grandmother's hand,
and on the steep staircase he kisses my lips.

Summer 1917

14

The mysterious spring still lay under a spell,
the transparent wind stalked over the mountains,
and the deep lake kept on being blue,—
a temple of the Baptist not made by hands.

You were frightened by our first meeting,
but I already prayed for the second, and now
the evening is hot, the way it was then . . .
How close the sun has come to the mountain.

You are not with me, but this is no separation:
to me each instant is—triumphant news.
I know there is such anguish in you
that you cannot say a single word.

Spring 1917

15

I hear the always-sad voice of the oriole
and I salute the passing of delectable summer.
With the hissing of a snake the scythe cuts down
the stalks, one pressed hard against another.

And the hitched-up skirts of the slender reapers
fly in the wind like holiday flags. Now if only
we had the cheerful ring of harness bells,
a lingering glance through dusty eyelashes.

I don't expect caresses or flattering love-talk,
I sense unavoidable darkness coming near,
but come and see the Paradise where together,
blissful and innocent, we once lived.

1917

16

You are an apostate: for a green island
you give away your native land,
our songs and our icons
and the pine tree over the quiet lake.

Why is it, you dashing man from Yaroslav,
if you still have your wits
why are you gaping at the beautiful red-heads
and the luxurious houses?

You might as well be sacrilegious and swagger,
finish off your orthodox soul,
stay where you are in the royal capital
and begin to love your freedom in earnest.

How does it happen that you come to moan
under my small high window?
You know yourself that waves won't drown you
and mortal combat leaves you without a scratch.

It's true that neither the sea nor battles
frighten those who have renounced Paradise.
That's why at the hour of prayer
you asked to be remembered.

1917
Slepnevo

Various Later Poems

17

Wild honey has the scent of freedom,
dust—of a ray of sun,
a girl's mouth—of a violet,
and gold—has no perfume.

Watery—the mignonette,
and like an apple—love,
but we have found out forever
that blood smells only of blood.

18

It is not with the lyre of someone in love
that I go seducing people.
The rattle of the leper
is what sings in my hands.

19
Tale of the Black Ring

1

Presents were rare things
coming from my grandmother, a Tartar;
and she was bitterly angry
when I was baptized.
But she turned kind before she died
and for the first time pitied me,
sighing: "Oh the years!
and here my young granddaughter!"
Forgiving my peculiar ways
she left her black ring to me.
She said: "It becomes her,
with this things will be better for her."

2

I said to my friends:
"There is plenty of grief, so little joy."
And I left, covering my face;
I lost the ring.
My friends said:
"We looked everywhere for the ring,
on the sandy shore,
and among pines near the small clearing."
One more daring than the rest
caught up with me on the tree-lined drive
and tried to convince me
to wait for the close of day.
The advice astonished me

and I grew angry with my friend
because his eyes were full of sympathy:
"And what do I need you for?
You can only laugh,
boast in front of the others
and bring flowers."
I told them all to go away.

3

Coming into my cheerful room
I called out like a bird of prey,
fell back on the bed
to remember for the hundredth time
how I sat at supper
and looked into dark eyes,
ate nothing, drank nothing
at the oak table,
how under the regular pattern of the tablecloth
I held out the black ring,
how he looked into my face,
stood up and stepped out onto the porch.

. . . .

They won't come to me with what they have found!
Far over the swiftly moving boat
the sails turned white,
the sky flushed pink.

1917–1936

20
On the Road

Though this land is not my own
I will never forget it,
or the waters of its ocean,
fresh and delicately icy.

Sand on the bottom is whiter than chalk,
and the air drunk, like wine.
Late sun lays bare
the rosy limbs of the pine trees.

And the sun goes down in waves of ether
in such a way that I can't tell
if the day is ending, or the world,
or if the secret of secrets is within me again.

1964

Notes

"The memory of sun weakens in my heart" . . . from *Evening*.
Line 15: Literally, "Maybe! This night will manage to come/winter."

"Evening hours at the desk" . . . from *Rosary*.
Line 3: Literally, "The mimosa smells of Nice and warmth."

"I know, I know the skis" . . . from *Rosary*.
Line 6: Literally, "removed by silence."
Line 8: Holes in the ice made by fishermen . . .

"The Guest" . . . from *Rosary*.
Line 13: Literally, "And his eyes gazing dimly . . ."
Lines 17 and 18: Literally, "Oh I know his bliss is to know (with stress, by force) and passionately . . ."

"There is a sacred, secret line" . . . from *White Flock*.
Line 1: Literally, ". . . in inloveness" . . . "being in love."
Line 3: Literally, ". . . even if lips blend . . ."
Line 5: Literally, ". . . friendship is impotent . . ."
Line 8: Literally, ". . . the slow languor of carnal passion."

"Like a white stone in a deep well" . . . from *White Flock*.

"Everything promised him to me . . ." from *White Flock*.
Line 10: Literally, ". . . that he would be friends with me."
Line 12: Literally, ". . . along the hot, stony path."

"Twenty-first. Night. Monday . . ." from *Plantain*.
Line 3: ". . . who knows why"—literally, ". . . what did he have to do that for?"
Line 8: Literally, ". . . they sing love songs."

"There is a certain hour every day" . . . from *Plantain*.
Line 3: Here translated as melancholy; in the Russian, *toska:* melancholy, yearning, boredom, sweet sadness, all at once. What is more, *toska* has a feminine gender. So *she* pulses like blood, *she's* warm like a sigh, etc., thereby making "sisters" of the speaker and the melancholy to which she addresses herself.

"We walk along the hard crest . . ." from *Plantain*.
In Russian the verb "walk" is delayed until line 4, and is coupled with an adjective meaning "soft" or "tender."
Line 8: Literally, ". . . the tinkling of your spurs."

"All day the crowd rushes . . ." from *Plantain*.
Lines 1 and 2: Literally, "And the whole day, turning frightened of its own gasps, in deadly agitation the crowd rushes."

"The mysterious spring . . ." from *Plantain*.
Line 8: Literally, ". . . how low the sun stands over the mountain."

"You are an apostate . . ." from *Plantain*.
Line 17: Literally, "Yes, neither the sea nor battles . . ."

"Wild honey has the scent of freedom . . ." from Struve, Vol. 2, p. 137. *Poems of Various Years*.
Line 4: Literally, ". . . and gold—of nothing."
Lines 5 and 6: Literally, "Of water smells the mignonette,/and of apple—love."
It seemed important to keep the abstractions—freedom and love—in parallel positions within their stanzas. I couldn't bring myself to say "Of water smells the mignonette . . ."—that's not English. So I left out the verb and invented "watery."

"It is not with the lyre of someone in love . . ." from Struve, Vol. 2, p. 139.

"Tale of the Black Ring . . ." from Struve, Vol. 1, p. 180.
For Akhmatova the gift of the ring was synonymous with the gift of song.
Line 3: Grandmother was Muslim and baptism was foreign to her belief.
Line 27: Literally, ". . . his eyes are tender."

"On the Road" from *Odd Number: Verses 1907–1964* (Struve, Vol. 1, p. 336.)
Lines 7 and 8: Literally, "and the pink body of pines/is naked in the sunset hour."

II

Gardens, the Church, and a Mountain

❧

"Good-by and Keep Cold"

The gloomiest garden chore I can think of is preparing the perennial beds for winter. The golden days of autumn—when chrysanthemums and asters still bloom, and a cricket or two still chirp in the long, lush grass that needs mowing one more time—those apple-fragrant days are gone, replaced by days when the ground never softens, but remains gray and buff and dry and hard—the ruts in the frozen drive seemingly turn to stone.

By now the mower is back in the barn, empty of gas and of life's noisy possibilities; I cover it with a tarp against bat droppings. Garden tools lean in the dark shed, everything idle, the raking and transplanting done. Our revels now are ended.

In October we cut the flower stalks to the ground and cart away the refuse. The undiseased stalks we pitch onto the compost pile; those flecked with mildew or black spot go over the edge of the ravine behind the barn—the horticultural equivalent of an automotive graveyard, the end of the line. Asparagus stalks rattle with the dryness of bamboo when I cut them down, a mournful sound. We gather up armfuls of long, straplike leaves of Siberian iris; moist, reddish peony stalks; woody hollyhock stems, taller than I am. We lay bare the crowns of the plants, and let them freeze deliberately.

Now that the ground is hard, perennials locked into the earth, it's time to mulch the long beds with chopped-up leaves and a top dressing of manure. Over it all we put cut boughs of pine to keep the brown coverlet in place, to keep the ground frozen, not to keep it warm, so that a mild spell won't tempt the plants into growth, only to be killed by the next cold weather. My red-haired stepdaughter,

43

Philippa, who majored in plant science, explained to me that the alternate freezing and thawing of plant cells, expansion and contraction, bursts the cells, producing what we call winterkill. Robert Frost wrote:

> No orchard's the worse for the wintriest storm:
> But one thing about it, it mustn't get warm.
> "How often already you've had to be told,
> Keep cold, young orchard, good-by and keep cold.

Now the last leaves are down, except for the thick, dark leaves of the oak and ghostly beech leaves that click in the breeze, and we're reduced to a subtler show of color—brown, gray, and buff, perhaps a little purple in the distance, and the black-green of moss, hemlock, and fir. To my eye these hues are more beautiful than the garish early autumn with its orange leaves—orange, the color of madness—and leaves the color of blood. Let hot life retire, grow still: November's colors are those of the soul.

Thanksgiving, with its reliable bounty, its reunions, its hours of perfumed air, is over, and the raking, the planting of bulbs, and the digging of root crops are finished for the year. The freezer and pantry shelves are as full as they are going to be: What we have done, we have done; and what we have left undone, we have left undone.

Silence and darkness grow apace, broken only by the crack of a hunter's gun in the woods. Songbirds abandon us so gradually that, until the day when we hear no birdsong at all but the scolding of a jay, we haven't fully realized that we are bereft—as after a death. Even the sun has gone off somewhere. By teatime the parlor is as black as the inside of a cupboard.

Reading after supper on the couch, I let my mind wander to the compost pile, bulging with leaves and stalks. I've turned it a few times since October, but the pile's hard surface no longer yields to the fork. Even the earthworms have retreated from the cold and closed the door behind them. There's an oven warm at the pile's center, but you have to take that on faith. Now we all come in, having put the garden to bed, and we wait for winter to pull a chilly sheet over its head.

The Moment of Peonies

It is the month of peonies—the week, the day, and the hour of peonies. In late March their red asparagus-like shoots began to push toward the intensely blue spring sky with its scudding clouds. Through April and May the stalks gained height and turned green; buds formed and swelled tantalizingly. Ants crawled over the veined globes with gathering excitement, and now, at last, comes the hot day after a warm rain when the flowers open. And we are blessed, we are undone by them.

Five years ago we made a big change in the yard here. We dug up the hosta lilies that grew along the porch, which had been planted when three or four large elms grew in the yard, shading the front garden. In the years since Dutch elm disease destroyed the trees, the hosta had been getting too much sun, burning up every summer.

So we moved the hosta to a raised bed under the maples (where the hummingbirds continue to patronize them), and that fall I planted seven peonies in their place—Festiva Maxima—from my favorite mail-order nursery in Connecticut. I dug labor-intensive holes for them, taking out the subsoil and replacing it with compost and peat. I added prodigious amounts of bone meal and mixed it up with the compost. I did everything right for these flowers, mulching them after the ground was frozen, fertilizing them in the spring when the shoots had grown a couple of inches, even drenching them with Captan, against fusarium wilt and against my principles. The first year they made a modest but respectable beginning, with three or four blossoms to a plant, and every year they have gained in stature.

This year the plants exceed every expectation. Suddenly they've come into their full adult beauty, not strapping, but statuesque—the beauty of women, as Chekhov says, "with plump shoulders" and with long hair held precariously in place by a few stout pins. They are white, voluminous, and here and there display flecks of raspberry red on the edges of their fleshy, heavily scented petals.

These are not Protestant-work-ethic flowers. They loll about in gorgeousness; they live for art; they believe in excess. They are not quite decent, to tell the truth. Neighbors and strangers slow their cars to gawk.

Yesterday violent thunderstorms battered Hillsborough county, to the south, and I heard on the car radio that three-quarter-inch hailstones were falling there. All I could think about was getting home to my peonies. I floored it and imagined myself saying to the man in the broad-brimmed tan felt hat, "But, officer, this *is* an emergency!" We in Merrimack county had no hail, as it turned out, but rain bent the heavy-headed flowers over their wire supports and shattered many blossoms.

This morning petals whiten the ground as if snow had fallen in the night or as if a swan had molted in the garden. The smaller, ancillary buds have yet to bloom, but the great display is over. Some gardeners pinch out these small side buds so that the plant's energy will go into a few huge blooms, but I never have the heart. At least my little ones are left—my debutantes.

I suppose if I had to declare a favorite flower, it would be peonies, and here I find myself in the moments just after their great, abandoned splurge. They seem like the diva in her dressing gown after the opera—still glistening, but spent. "Death is the mother of beauty," the poet Wallace Stevens tells us. Maybe never again will all the elements conspire to make another such marvelous moment of flowers. I'm glad I wasn't away from home or, as the Buddhists say, asleep.

The Phantom Pruner

Sensible people grow green beans. I grow peonies, campanula, roses, lilies, astilbe, bee balm. No matter how many flowers, there are never enough, and I harbor Napoleonic tendencies toward floral expansion. When we cut some maple trees away from the barn foundation, partly to protect the sills, and partly to keep the constant dripping and consequent lichen off the shingles, I saw an opportunity to expand my empire. Into the sandy loam went Siberian iris, poppies, sunflowers, flowering shrubs, daylilies, and some iris that clashed with the colors in my back border. I even put in a few tomato plants, lettuce, basil, and Italian parsley. Why didn't I just let the farmer who hays for us cut closer to the barn? I'd have saved myself hours of digging, a few encounters with poison ivy, and some nights on the heating pad.

The balance of power in a garden is never the same from year to year. You never grow the same garden twice, try as you may. The feverfew gets weedy and greedy and overtakes a quarter of the bed under the kitchen window. A flower gardener must be ruthless. Sometimes you must pull invaders out of the ground, not to replant them, but to throw them on the compost pile. It is troubling to decide what shall live and what shall die—to do your best for some flower and to yank another summarily out of the ground.

Another life-and-death summer chore is clearing brush, and trimming the lower limbs of trees, something I do when my husband is away, because he hates to see trees cut. He calls me an arboricide. I noticed, however, that when several trees had to be cut down and several others trimmed severely for his satellite dish to be installed, his Joyce Kilmer inclinations vanished instantly.

Our old white lilacs lean over his car, dropping sap every spring until the Honda looks as if it's been driven through a vat of used motor oil. I get out the long-handled pruners and the fiendishly sharp Japanese pruning saw and cut back the overhang, hoping he won't notice. If I didn't limb the lower branches of the maples, you couldn't see to pull out of the drive. I do it when Don is out of town, or when the Red Sox are playing—same thing.

I wish I could look at trees in our yard without thinking of changing their contours. Untrammeled nature is beautiful enough, yet shapeliness—*made* beauty—counts for more. I cut down the ash tree that's growing up through the branches of the old pear. I prune the lowest branches of the pear to make it less earthbound. I'm well aware that my efforts and tastes will pass away with my stewardship here.

Don loves old roses. We have plenty, but a maple that my stepson planted is beginning to overshadow them. Someday when Don's at the dentist I'll take the lower branches of the maple, or it's good-bye roses. These old white and pink flowers have grown stubbornly next to Route 4 for at least a hundred years. Every winter the plow breaks them and heaps salt on them. One day I came back from town to find that the state road crew had sheared them off completely. I walked around briefly, holding my head, then got busy: I top-dressed them with bone meal and manure and watered them. The next year they were fine, if short.

This summer I acquired a pruning saw on a pole, so I can really reach up there. I've discovered a small stand of Siberian dogwood and yellow birch behind the satellite dish. Gradually I'm uncovering them, cutting away regiments of oak and maple saplings, and lilac suckers. Alas, there's one large overhanging oak limb that no amount of wishing or reaching will eliminate. I think for Christmas I'll ask Santa for some tree work; I'll point and he can cut.

It's not just more flowers I want, it's more light, more air for flowers, more sun for cheerfulness. A person gets her fill of shade-loving plants. She wants swaying hollyhocks, clove-scented pinks, and lavender plants as big as bushes. She doesn't care so much about conquering Moscow as she does about having a comely pear tree and a hundred white daffodils that glow after dusk against the unpainted boards of an old barn.

Notes of a Novice Hiker

One day last spring I went tramping with neighbors over Ragged Mountain in south central New Hampshire, where I live. The trees had only begun to leaf out, allowing the sun to penetrate to the forest floor; dog-tooth violets and mayflowers bloomed everywhere among tender ferns. I walked with friends whom I encounter almost every morning on New Canada Road, they on their morning run from the Danbury side of the mountain, and I on mine from the West Andover side. My dog Gus—a timid soul at heart, but inclined to be fierce when surprised—always growls and lunges at Judy and Steve. Dog biscuits and sweet talk have had no effect. This is how we became acquainted—as Judy and Steve made large circles around us. I offered profuse apologies.

Although it is virtually my backyard, I had not been far up Ragged since the day I got lost there alone. The streambed I intended to follow down to the road came abruptly to an end, the water disappearing underground; the sun began to go down. That day, I found my way back to Route 4, chastened, by listening for the sound of traffic, and coming out of the woods a mile or so away from the house. So much for solitary ramblings on a mountain without a compass, even a mountain that rises behind one's own house and barn.

The Gordons had the kindness to ask me along on their early spring hike despite our tense encounters. I left my little psychopath at home. The hills were rich with a hundred greens, everything waxing, leaves the size of the nail on my little finger. A small, deep violet butterfly jigged and jagged between flowers. The air was warm, but a cool breath rose from the streambeds, still muddy from the spring melt.

We climbed directly under the Ragged Mountain ski lift, bore south-east at the top, and picked up a series of dubious trails, emerging about three hours later behind Proctor Academy in Andover.

Judy and Steve are experienced hikers, having climbed all the peaks in the state over 4,000 feet. They said they'd be walking up Mount Washington before long; would I like to come? I've climbed Kearsarge often, and Cardigan, but they were asking me to climb the great-grandmother mountain—6,288 feet. A Cog Railway runs up and down the western slope. Years ago from my seat on the train I saw hikers coming out of the woods, looking weary but triumphant, and I thought, "There's something I'll never be strong enough to do." I thought of them as a different species of human being. This was B.G.—before Gus—before I began daily walks up Ragged Mountain with the dog, and before the walking escalated to running to evade the blackflies and mosquitoes.

I asked Steve how long the climb would take.

"Four and a half hours up, three and a half hours down," he replied.

"Do you really think you could get me up there?"

"No problem."

Some weeks later a note appeared in my mailbox: "Hikeogram #1: Judy and I could climb Mt. Washington either of two weekends in June (9th/23rd). If you'd like to go R.S.V.P. Steve." Sometimes in life you let things happen to you: I called them.

I bought some light hikers. I wanted the teal and purple kind that gleam in the pages of the L.L. Bean catalog, but of course everybody buys those first, and the only ones left in my size were General Schwarzkopf boots. I put flower decals on them, and crazy laces, and to break them in, I wore them around the yard as I cut brush on the hillside and mowed our long, sandy banks. I'd bought a backpack after climbing Cardigan, deciding that I'd carried neither enough water, nor warm clothes for the windy ledges at the summit. I like to sit in comfort for a while, having earned the view.

In Hikeogram #2 Steve provided me with a list of things I'd need for our June hike: a first aid kit, moleskin, food, three changes of clothes, including winterwear, a bungee cord, extra shoelaces, a ten-foot length of rope. My heart sank when I read about the rope. I never could bring myself to ask what it might be for.

All week my excitement burgeoned. Either I would be dead by Sunday evening, or more alive than I had ever been before. Trust the Gordons, my instinct told me. They know what they are doing, and you are in reasonable shape for a forty-four-year-old poet.

On the clear, cool morning of the 23rd we arrived at the base of the Ammonoosuc Trail by eight. The next hours were among the most ecstatic of my life. First there's the easy walk to the Gem Pool, with bunchberry, laurel, and wild honeysuckle blooming all around; bright, tender shoots of new growth on the pines and firs as shockingly beautiful as a baby's ear; mica glinting underfoot. Suddenly you come to the clearing where the pool gleams under the falls, the deep end slanting down precipitously, rocks at the bottom clearly visible. A family sat by the water eating lunch. We lolled about for a few minutes, splashed our faces and necks to cool ourselves, took a few pictures, and savored the place. Suddenly Judy stood up, slapping her knees. "Well, the honeymoon's over!" We climbed granite stairs for the next two and a half hours. . . .

In the conditioning class I take, we've learned, when pain becomes intense, to blow out our breath forcefully, like women in labor, then to inhale deeply and slowly. Blowing goes against the natural tendency to hold your breath when you are uncomfortable, but it helps on an arduous climb. Judy is a nurse in a midwife's practice in Concord. She kept saying to me, "You're doing fine, you're doing great!" and I half expected a miraculous delivery along the trail. Judy and Steve's breathing was more demure.

Every now and then Steve pulled me briskly with one hand up a steep outcropping of granite. Judy made it without help. Occasionally I'd gasp, "Pit stop!" and we'd pause for a mouthful of cold water from our packs, and some food. I'd brought dried apricots mixed with almonds and M&M's, and they were ambrosial. The guidebook warns against drinking from the mountain streams, for beaver scat sometimes pollutes the water, but we broke the rule once and "kissed the water" about an hour's walk above the Gem Pool.

There were few people on the trail the day of our ascent. We came across perhaps twelve other hikers—a couple of teenagers in short-sleeved knit shirts, with no packs, who would have been in serious trouble had the weather changed suddenly. They climbed past us as if they were walking down Main Street. But Steve had warned me, and everything I've read about the mountain says to prepare for any conceivable turn in the weather, even in high summer. Several plaques along the path mark places where hikers died of exposure, caught in sudden storms, not only in winter.

We climbed past a young woman who clearly wasn't going to make it to the top, and would have all she could do to get back to the trailhead. I heard her say, "I don't know what's the matter with me. I'm shaking all over." She lay near the path, pallid and sweating profusely, her two slim, hard-looking male companions smoking, and talking quietly between themselves, looking impatient.

Just as I began to wonder if my knees were going to hold out, the Lakes of the Clouds Hut came into view. It's not beautiful from the back—propane tanks and sewage pipes are the first thing you see—but it's a welcome sight. Inside, we changed from our light, wet clothes—everything down to our underwear was soaked from effort—into dry, warmer clothes. We had a cup of hot, intensely sweet cocoa. A few essentials are for sale here, moleskin for blistered feet, pocket knives, T-shirts, wool socks.

I couldn't believe what I had seen—the cold cataracts, firs and spruces becoming dwarfer and more contorted as we approached the timberline, the glinting bulges of granite shot through with mica, the vistas of the Ammonoosuc Ravine and the summit, smoke from the Cog Railway drifting overhead. I looked around at the other climbers in the room. Not one of them under thirty; all of them well-equipped and fit. This is a different crowd from the one on Kearsarge or Cardigan, leaner and more ascetic. One woman who sat alone at a table must have been in her seventies, mottled skin hanging from her thin, muscular legs after years of exposure to the sun. She looked as sturdy as the table she leaned on.

Abruptly on leaving the hut we found ourselves above the treeline. A warning sign says to turn back immediately in case of bad weather. Here, a sudden sleet or a snow squall would make the rocky footing impossible. Cold, wet, and immobile hikers become vulnerable to hypothermia within minutes, and above the treeline there is nothing to burn to make a fire. Lightning could strike with no place to shelter. One could easily get lost in the fog, for the blazes on the rocks are hard to see at a distance, and the cairns are many feet apart, and further, there's no clearly worn path underfoot, only stones. "Turn back without shame" says the *Appalachian Mountain Club White Mountain Guide.*

But we climbed on the rare absolutely clear day, just the odd cloud drifting benignly overhead to make big, slow shadows on the ancient hills and ravines. We could see the summit now, and the sight provided me with ambition I'd begun to need. Everywhere lichen grew on rocks—mostly greenish, but there were also black lichens, some furry, some frilly, and alpine flowers and sedges—found also in Labrador—so small they'd be easily missed. Among the mostly granite stones were big chunks of quartz, looking like ice, with brown, beard-like lichen growing on them, and, rarely, a red stone, usually smaller than a volleyball, smoother than the other stones, the color of marble pillars you see in Italian churches. What terrible and wonderful forces brought these stones to this place, imported these tiny, pertinacious flowers from Labrador? I loved the body of the earth that day as never before, our mother's great stony flanks, her conifer-covered slopes looking soft, somehow, in the distance.

Now we balanced from rock to rock, taxing in its own way, but requiring less strength because the vertical rise had moderated. "You're doing great," Judy kept saying. The antennae of the summit building rose before us, then the buildings themselves. Suddenly we stood among bundled hikers and tourists dressed in cotton resort wear who had just stepped off the Cog Railway into 38-degree temperatures with a 20-mile-an-hour wind. A bronze circle marks the absolute summit, and my friends propelled me up there, a little dazed, insisting that I step on it first. Judy touched it with the toe of her boot, having stood on that spot many times. Steve too made quick work of it.

We went inside for lunch, and to change clothes again, for we were soaked again. I had a bowl of bisque, with large floating chunks of tomato and a simple bag of oyster crackers—school-lunch line fare—but I was so cold and wet that the soup tasted better to me than anything I have ever eaten in Florence or Rome. I was so happy that I hardly knew what to do with myself.

I had planned all along to take the Railway down. We had climbed hard for five hours, and I knew I didn't have another four in me. I called my husband, who would retrieve me at the base, to tell him that I'd most likely be on the 3:30 train. After lunch, Steve and Judy didn't linger, but put on their packs and headed over the edge of the hill. I felt a brief moment of desolation, but I know my limits— their locus in my middle-aged knees—and so I climbed onto the blessed old rattling smoky train, standing room only, looking wistfully at the cracked green leather seats for half an hour until I sat down in the aisle, since all the blood in my body seemed to be collecting in my feet. I couldn't see the Great Gulf, but I listened to the other passengers' exclamations while I studied the scarlet toenails of a woman wearing high-heeled sandals, and admired the fittings of the old train. May no one ever change the tongue-in-groove paneling, the cracked seats, the worn brass handles on the backs of the seats. In her heyday the train was elegant; now her glory is diminished, but she still does her job.

In September we plan to climb the mountain again, going up Boott Spur to the Davis Path. I've been doing wind sprints uphill, and leg lifts with weights to strengthen my knees. In one of the remote closets of our farmhouse I found an old walking stick that seems made for me. I've tried it already on Cardigan, and it protected my knees on the way down. Since Judy is a nurse, and since I plan to equip myself with elastic kneeguards, I may disappear over the ridge of the hill with the Gordons in September, letting the Cog Railway chug along without me. I suppose that reaching the car, warm from being closed all day, as the late afternoon sun slants through the pines and birches, would make me about as happy as a human being can get.

South Danbury Church Fair (1990)

Wedges of pie on their paper plates cover one whole end of the canopied trestle table: lemon meringue, pecan, blueberry, apple, peach, chocolate cream, raspberry . . . Every crust is crimped in a different way, the sign of authentic pie. There are baked beans—again every pot different, made with all sizes, shapes, and colors of beans. I've noticed that people have passionate opinions about beans.

There's a big basket of homemade raised rolls, and brown bread that's been steamed in coffee cans; there are salads of every hue; casseroles—the obligatory macaroni and cheese, tuna fish, brown rice with tofu, a pan of lasagna big enough for a regiment; homemade ice cream—cherry, grape nut, coffee; and milk, or ice water, or strong coffee to drink.

This is the South Danbury Church Fair Supper, served at five o'clock sharp on the second Saturday in July.

If you come early, you can meander among tables on the lawn, where the women of the church sell fancywork—knitted baby booties, gingham aprons with embroidered pockets and ties; baked goods—muffins, penuche, all kinds of breads, pies, cookie bars; white elephants—books, plants, fabrics someone didn't get around to making up, beaded evening bags, fly swatters, and antiquated ski boots; grabs—toys wrapped mysteriously so the kids can't tell what they have until they tear open the paper. It's usually hot, genuinely hot, and under the apple tree there's a big galvanized tub with sodas bobbing in icy water.

After the supper, at six thirty or so, we have an auction, accompanied by all kinds of foolishness. The auctioneer puts the string mop on his head like a wig. Someone buys every record Johnny Cash ever made for $2.00. My husband works on the auction committee. He delivers the goods and collects the money, the big pockets of his carpenter's apron bulging with ones. All this transpires on a hill, and by seven-thirty he has turned the color of a pomegranate. The auctioneer's face is only slightly redder. Everything sells, almost. A bowling ball, a length of stovepipe, and a pair of crutches, despite the auctioneer's repeated attempts to sell them, will greet worshipers in the church vestibule the next morning.

The gathering at the supper tables under the trees, and at the auction afterward, constitutes a union of friends, a fellowship. Marge Cornell, who used to keep the West Andover store, comes to our auction all the way from Boscawen, and catches up on everyone's recent news. Jokes abound, and reminiscences. There's always a new baby or two, a new face consisting of many faces, a new soul. Last year, while I was counting forks and cutting pies, my husband and our son-in-law's parents from Warner were showing off our grandchild, Allison Harriman Smith, about to be one year old.

On Sunday morning, the day after the fair, all the heavy picnic tables and the big trestle table and canopy have to be returned to their owners, trash cleared from the barrels, and the barrels carted away. Our men, few of them young, work a little beyond their strength, and I worry for them. The congregation moves in slow motion that morning, and sometimes we eliminate our usual coffee hour after the service. On the other hand, sometimes we eat leftover pie.

On Monday afternoon several of us meet to count the sticky coins and bills. A table fan oscillates on the floor, so that the bills won't fly out of their piles. First we count the income from each table separately, and then we put the money together and count again. The fair is hot and hard work, but in one afternoon fifteen or twenty people, parishioners and friends, make enough to pay the oil and light bills for the year.

Now the fair's over for another year, the worn grass has straightened up again, the coins are rolled and banked, and soon enough Labor Day will be upon us, the sermon punctuated by the constant susurrus of tires, cars loaded with bicycles and camping gear headed back to the city. May the person who acquired the complete Johnny Cash library live and thrive, and come back to us next year on the second Saturday in July.

Childhood, When You Are in It . . .*

Childhood, when you are in it, seems to last forever. Summer, for instance, seems endless. Whatever happens in the moment displaces past and future entirely. What happened to me in childhood was my grandmother, father's mother. The central psychic fact of that time was Grandmother's spiritual obsession, and her effort to secure me in her religious fold.

Often when Mother and Father went somewhere without us, my brother and I stayed with Grandma in her big house on State Street in Ann Arbor, where she took in University of Michigan students as boarders. Grandfather had died. I have no memory of him, except of sitting on his bony knees after he had had strokes. The stubble on his face was white, and a cane lay beside his chair, which smelled vaguely of urine. I was afraid of his incapacity, but not of him. When he died Grandmother began to say something she would have to say for the next twenty-nine years, for she lived to be one hundred and three: "I wish God would take me so I can be with George and Mother."

Dora Baldwin Kenyon was tall and slim, with a handsome build, and a mournful expression. I loved to stand behind her when she sat at her dressing table, brushing her long gray hair, then braiding it for the night. She used cold cream on her face, and the smell overpowered me. Her house in general smelled of Ivory soap and gas from the kitchen range—a different smell from our house, which had, it seemed to me, no smell.

---

*Jane left this unfinished essay without a title.

I might have been seven or eight when my grandmother first said to me, opening her eyes wide, and then wider, "The body is the temple of the Holy Ghost." We were sitting in the dark living room, dark because the shades were kept half-drawn, and the sheer curtains were never pulled back. "The body is the temple . . ." What could this mean? and where was my brother? I don't remember his presence as I heard this astonishing declaration. Had he been there, we surely would have exchanged looks, and talked, later, about what she meant.

I knew about ghosts from my comic books—*Casper the Friendly Ghost.* Casper looked like a sheet draped over a round shape, perhaps a ball, and he had a face much like Frosty the Snowman's—button nose, black shining eyes, and a contented, even benevolent expression. Casper was prankish, but never vicious.

I knew that Grandmother had said something solemn, and I knew that somehow *my* body was under discussion. Something was going on inside me without my knowledge or consent. She was urging me to do or be a certain way, but what way? Didn't you have to die to be a ghost? And what did "holy" mean? The one encouraging thing was that Casper was friendly, and I deduced from this that the Holy Ghost would be friendly too.

Dora's favorite hymn was, "Onward Christian Soldiers, marching as to war . . ." She played it often on Father's baby grand piano, which he left with her when we moved to a house too small to contain it. There were always hymnbooks on the piano, but never Bach or Beethoven or Chopin. The piano bench, under its lid, was groaning with hymnals and religious sheet music.

Grandmother began every day with devotions from *The Upper Room,* a brief reading from the scriptures, and a prayer: "Bless this food to our good, and us to thy service." Only then would we eat together thick pieces of her homemade bread, toasted, and drink orange juice, which she squeezed herself from the unlikeliest-looking small, greenish oranges. The juice glasses were flared at the rim, and had green garlands on them.

Then it would be time to go up to the students' rooms, to make their beds and empty their ashtrays and wastebaskets. What a pungent smell the leavings of their cigarettes made, a smell totally foreign to me. (My parents did not smoke.) I thought there must be something about getting educated that made a person smell like that. As we worked, Grandmother talked about hell, a lake of fire, burning endlessly, or about the Second Coming of Christ, which would put an end to the world as I knew it.

Once we had filled a paper grocery bag with their trash, we went down to the small cellar stove in which she burned the household refuse. She struck a wooden match and held the flame to an empty envelope, twisted to make a wick, then held the wick to three or four places in the stove so the fire would be sure to start. I watched the fire move inexorably, and thought about burning forever, not burning and then going out, but burning eternally—the fate of boys and girls who sassed their parents, or gave grudgingly to the offering at Sunday school, or played with cards. And of course that would be the fate of those who gambled or drank. I myself had played with cards, and my parents had a scotch and soda every night before dinner. I lived in terror of letting it slip.

I don't think my parents realized that my sojourns with Grandma had become religious retreats. She told me about Christ and the second coming, which she anticipated more eagerly than anyone I have ever known. Jesus would come out of the clouds, or, as my imagination had it, he'd walk down a sunbeam like a ramp, to judge us—rather like Santa Claus, as I understood *him*. And if we'd been good children, our names would appear in God's book of life, a large book indeed, but, I supposed, God would have a lap sufficient to accommodate it. (I conceived of God as a larger, gray-haired Jesus—Jesus

Senior, so to speak.) If we hadn't been good children, it would be better never to have been born at all. The question for her was not do we love God, and our neighbors as ourselves, but have we obeyed, out of fear, his commandments. And have we obeyed Grandma's personal amendments to the law of Moses: Thou shalt not dance, or wear nail polish; thou shalt not wear nylons too early in adolescence; thou shalt not play games of chance . . .

At the moment of Christ's coming, she went on, two women would be grinding at the mill, and God would take one to be with him in heaven and leave the other standing alone. Two men would be plowing in the field. One would turn back to his house for something he thought he needed. Woe to him! Two would be sleeping in the same bed (I knew that there was something fishy about two in the same bed anyway), and God would choose only one!

Jesus might reappear at any time, at night, even, as her last example showed. Like a thief in the night! This was confusing, because thieves are bad people, but I got a picture of great haste, furtiveness, and I was quite certain that Jesus would not wait while I fumbled with curlers and pajama buttons. It was hard for me to fall asleep at 925 South State Street. When I was at home, I had no fear that Jesus would come in the night to judge my life.

By the age of nine or ten I began to resent the power my religious fears held over me. One day at school I did something that would either end my life on the spot, or prove to me that Grandma was wrong about God. I was angry with my friend, and drawing myself up yelled, "Goddamit, Joanie!" A shudder went through me as I said the words. I expected to die in the dust under the swing I was sitting in. I heard only the sound of the wind, but I knew I was lost; I had sinned against the Holy Spirit. God had spared my life so I could suffer. This was the beginning of eternity. It was only when I began to suffer that I entered eternity.

Not long after, I attempted another disobedience. I was unhappy in my one-room country school, where the teacher didn't like me, and I didn't respect her, and there was no hope of evading her for the next three years. One day I felt that Miss Sikima had been unjust. I opened the heavy gate of the Cyclone fence that enclosed the yard of Foster School, Ann Arbor Township, No. 16 Fractional. I closed the gate behind me with a clank as the post fell into the concrete fitting, and I headed for home—perhaps a two-mile walk along gravel roads. But with every step I lost courage, and when I heard the schoolbell ring, and the cries of my playmates were replaced by the rustling of leaves, I couldn't take another step, and I turned back, and was punished for coming in late from recess. Miss Sikima had broken me, she and Grandma. I had neither the courage to rebel, nor an obedient heart.

My fall from grace continued. In her living room Grandma kept a blue pottery box, hand-painted with flowers—not formal and fine, but rough, *fauve*. One of her boarders had given it to her. I thought it was the most beautiful thing in her house. She had asked me not to handle it. One day, when she was out of the room, I picked it up to look at it more closely. (I was already myopic.) The glaze was crazed, and this seemed to me most marvelous—like a net, like the net of the fishermen who became Christ's disciples. While turning it this way and that, I dropped the lid and broke it. Sick, I gathered the pieces and took them to Grandma in the kitchen. She was angry, but not unfairly angry, I thought. She mended the box with glue, clumsily, which exacerbated my pain, and put it back in place. I tried never to look in that direction any more.

When Grandma was in her late seventies she and two of her sisters, Nina and Carrie, took a trip to the Holy Land. Grandmother had lived frugally all her life, and the family was astonished by her plans; I have her travel diary and a few pictures of her standing with her sisters and the rest of the tour group on the steps of a TWA prop airliner. They went first to Rome, where they visited the Vatican and

Saint Peter's, the Catacombs and the Forum, and then to Corinth, in Greece, where Saint Paul established one of the early churches. Finally they went to Jerusalem, and walked over the stony hills, thinking of their Lord. When she returned she spoke to the King's Daughters Circle of her church about her experience. Now, like Simeon, she was ready to depart in peace. But she was years away from departure.

I lay under Grandmother's spell, but my brother, who somehow threw off her influence, became a museum-goer and a lover of natural science. There was a natural history museum on the University of Michigan campus, and sometimes I would go with Reuel so he could show me his latest discoveries. Among these was an exhibit of Egyptian mummies. This was the first suggestion that there might be a scenario for life after death other than Grandma's. The mummies and their shining regalia lightened for me the burden of the mysteries of life and death. Death looked like a manageable business—you packed what you would need, as for any trip.

By the time I was in high school I grew contemptuous of religion and the people I knew who practiced it, although I took great pains to hide this development from Grandmother. I threw off the notion that I was sinful by nature, having read about Rousseau's noble savage, and feeling akin to him. I announced to my parents that one could not be a Christian and an intellectual, and that I would no longer attend church.

I sampled the Unitarian church on Washtenaw Avenue's Fraternity Row, but I rejected even that as too formal, too organized. I'm not a joiner, I thought, with considerable satisfaction. Nature will be my God, and I'll be a good person simply because it is the right thing to do.

I still saw Grandmother often. I had my driver's license, and I used to take her grocery shopping at the A&P. Sometimes on Sundays the whole family would visit—Mother and Father, Reuel and I. We sat on the scratchy maroon horsehair furniture, which made a peculiar pattern on the backs of one's legs. "Put a pillow to your back," Grandma would say. By this time she read her Bible, tattered by use, with a large, rectangular magnifying glass. Going home in the car afterward, my brother and I would imitate with savage accuracy her pronouncements about the Second Coming. I still felt sinful when we mocked Grandma in the car.

Although she lived only on Social Security, Grandmother always remembered our birthdays, and she always added, in her large and squarish script, a verse from the Bible. My brother and I didn't know where to look when we opened the cards in front of her. She lived on terribly little (my father joked that his mother could make cookies out of coffee grounds and bacon grease) so that she could send frequent contributions to the radio evangelists she listened to all day. She never doubted that God would take care of her as he takes care of the sparrows of the field.

In 1972 I married. Grandmother gave me a King James Bible bound in white leather as a wedding present. In the front was a page of dedication: Presented to _____, by _____ in _____. After the "by" she had managed to write a sloping "Grandma." I filled in the rest for her. Years passed, and the thin, gilt-edged pages remained stuck together, the cover immaculate.

❧

In 1975 my husband and I came to rural New Hampshire for the academic year, Don taking leave from the English Department at the University of Michigan. Much to my surprise, on the Sunday morning of our first week here, Don said, "I suppose we ought to go to church." We were living in the farmhouse where his mother and his grandmother had been born, and his ancestors had been among the founders of the South Danbury Church in 1867. Grudgingly I put on stockings and a skirt. The cousins were happy to see us in the last pew, but they did not seem surprised. The minister, Dr. Jack Jensen, happened to quote Rainer Maria Rilke in his sermon that week and how I did perk up then. We discovered that Jack often quoted poetry in his sermons.

We loved the solitude and silence of weekdays, combined with the coming together on Sunday. We began to attend church every Sunday. And in 1976 we decided to leave Ann Arbor, and move to the farm.

Something unlooked-for began to happen. Beyond the social pleasures I took from church, I started to take comfort from the prayer of confession and the assurance of pardon. I was twenty-nine years old; by now it was clear to me that I wasn't a good person all the time. I was sometimes irritable, selfish, and slow to forgive. It eased my mind to acknowledge my failings and start over.

Even in the years of my apostasy I never doubted that God exists, and that I exist in relation to God. I doubted everything else that Grandmother ever told me, but never that. Reverend Jensen had something to work with.

When I told him that the thought of reading the Bible by starting at page one daunted me, he suggested I begin with the New Testament, loaning me Mark's Gospel with William Barclay's commentary. Mark starts right in with the miracles and the parables, and I think Jack had me begin there because it was the direct way into the life and teachings of Christ. I read the other Gospels, loving John, the most mystical, best of all. I read the Acts of the Apostles, describing the early days of the church and Saint Paul's missionary journeys. I got to know this Saint Paul for myself, the passionate evangelist, turned from active persecutor of Christ. I read the Epistles, the Prophets, the Psalms.

I joined the church—Don had been a member since childhood—and watched in horror at the next annual meeting as the membership elected me church treasurer. I didn't know how to balance a check-book. Fourteen years later I am still the treasurer, and I have learned that the directions for balancing a checkbook are printed on the back of the bank statement. I've never overdrawn the account.

I was, and I am, disturbed by the sexism of the church, and the language of the church, and I began to search for the feminine in the Trinity. I read the women mystics, [Saint Teresa, Julian of Nor-wich,]* and I am still not satisfied with the beginning of the Lord's prayer, but this prayer has come to seem necessary to me, as Com-munion is necessary.

In 1980 I had an experience that changed my understanding com-pletely, changed my way of being in the world.

---

*The essay is unfinished. See the introduction.

Jane left a blank for "the women mystics," and I have supplied two whom she read and spoke of. Her fourteen years of being treasurer of our church, in one sentence here, puts this essay in 1991.

Gabriel's Truth

Italian Renaissance painting often shows the Virgin holding her place in the book she was reading when the angel broke in upon her—a curious anachronism as the ur-Mary was unlikely to have been reading a bound book. In any case, Mary stops reading and listens to Gabriel's outlandish news. The lives of God's holy ones are subject to major interruptions. I think of Simone Martini's depiction of the Annunciation. In many paintings of the period Mary draws back from Gabriel in trepidation, but I know of no other picture in which sorrow, fear, and even belligerence appear so clearly. The corners of her mouth turn downward. *Get away from me!*

But love was working in her, and in the faith which overturns fear she replied: "Behold the handmaid of the Lord: be it unto me according to thy word." How I love Martini's glimpse of Mary in the moments just before she brings herself to say *yes*.

Had Gabriel not appeared to Joseph in a dream, telling him that his betrothed was to be the mother of Jesus by the Holy Ghost, Mary might have been stoned to death as an adulteress. Shall we say that her pregnancy was an embarrassment: she bore the embarrassment.

She bore the surprise and discomfort of giving birth in a barn, the appearance of visitors who were complete strangers, and she bore the furtive, uncomfortable travel with a newborn to evade Herod's wrath. Already life was irregular for Mary, Joseph, and the baby.

Then, at Jesus' circumcision, Simeon said to Mary: "Behold this child is set for a sign which shall be spoken against; (Yea, a sword shall pierce through thy own soul also) . . ." There was going to be trouble unspecified. Gabriel's truth had been sketchy.

How did it feel to be the mother of a boy, who, when he was twelve, slipped away from his parents on the way from Jerusalem to Nazareth and disappeared for three days? (It was not the last time he would disappear for three days . . .) Mary and Joseph turned back to find him in the temple, holding forth among the elders. "Son, why hast thou thus dealt with us? Behold thy father and I have sought thee sorrowing." And what a sharp reply the boy gave: "How is it that ye sought me; wist ye not that I must be about my Father's business?" Her son, and not her son.

And for Joseph, also, these were hard words. "My Father's business . . ." (Later Christ would say, "Who is my mother, and who are my brethren?" when told that Mary desired a word with him.) Jesus was in the world, but not of it. The ordinary small contentments of domestic life eluded the Holy Family. This was the price of having God in the house. The episode in the temple finished Joseph: He is never heard from again in the narrative of Jesus' life, and tradition assumes that Joseph died not long after their equivocal reunion. Mary, however, followed Christ through everything—through his scrapes with the religious establishment, through the humiliation and apparent defeat on the cross. She never failed in her love for Jesus, no matter what personal disappointment or horror it led to.

Jesus performed his first miracle, if not for his mother, at least in her presence. They were together at a marriage feast in Cana when Mary observed that the wine was running low. And Jesus replied (before more or less doing his mother's bidding), "Woman, what have I to do with thee? Mine hour is not yet come." He meant that *he* was the wine, the wine of the new covenant, the blood which would be spilled. He knew it, and, as we read, even we know it, but Mary could only have been puzzled and perhaps hurt by the remark. Doubtless she pondered it in her heart.

Gabriel had told Mary that her son would be great beyond all measure, the son of the Highest, that his reign over the house of Jacob would have no end. He didn't warn her that Jesus would be in constant danger, that he would alienate his family in the service of greater love, that he would have no place to lay his head, that he would be betrayed by a close friend, arrested, mocked, scourged, and crucified between thieves.

Christ's destiny emerged to Mary's confusion and torment, and yet she accompanied her son everywhere, believing, hoping, against appearances, in Gabriel's truth. She chose not to spare herself any sorrow. John tells us that she "stood by the cross." What power and dignity those words reveal.

Mary teaches us to trust God always, to live in hope, to respond with love to whatever happens, to give and not count the cost, to be faithful in the worst circumstances. She teaches us, women and men alike, not to insist on ourselves, on our own comforts and satisfactions. And she shows us, finally, that her strenuous love was able to defeat death.

Blessed be Mary, the mother of our Lord, who suffered so sharply for our good.

III

Talking to Neighbors

❦

Columns for *The Concord Monitor*

Edna Powers

Wilmot. We live on Rte. 4 between Andover and Danbury, or, more accurately, in the small triangle of Wilmot that juts across Rte. 4, an area referred to variously as W. Andover, E. Wilmot and, once, in the *New York Times,* as "the curving wasteland of Rte. 4" (That was around primary time the year Carter was defeated). We have a Danbury mailing address and an Andover telephone exchange, and we pay taxes to Wilmot.

We can't go out for won ton soup at 2 A.M., that is true, but look what we've got: mountains, each a different color; birches, the most sentimental of trees; whippoorwills, the ultimate early risers. Unlike the *Times* reporter, I never tire of driving this stretch, peering over the fence to see if my neighbor's peas are up, or noting the sign "Beagle Puppies for Sale" that goes up every now and then, the "S" of "Sale" perpetually backwards.

Maybe the ice has gone out since you last looked, or the red-wings have come back, or the fiddleheads have begun to straighten their necks. There's plenty going on.

Our place can boast its people, too. "It's hard to write about goodness," my husband said when I mentioned that I planned to write about Edna Powers. Edna, who was born and lived here all her life, died suddenly, unexpectedly, on Good Friday afternoon.

Edna was a Democrat—an endangered species up this way—and not shy about it either. You never had to guess how she felt about anything. Edna was the only one to stand up in a town meeting all those years ago to say that the possibility of pollution made her go against the location of a dump in South Danbury. (South Danbury, and the

South Danbury Christian Church, is the epicenter of our region.) And didn't we have a mess from manganese, the rust from tin cans, just as she foresaw? The Jack Wells Brook turned bright orange, and Eagle Pond, and the top of the Blackwater River.

There isn't an institution in the town that won't be diminished by her absence—the Danbury School, the PTA, Blazing Star Grange, Old Home Day committee, South Danbury Church, King's Daughters Circle . . .

Is it possible to have Church Fair Supper on the second Saturday in July without Edna's Red Velvet Cake? I mean it was *red.* And if you were feeling depraved you could put a scoop of hand-cranked ice cream on top. She'd probably taken a turn at that, too.

Donations to the church in her memory keep coming. How to calculate, how to quantify the value of a person to a place . . . that outright wicked giggle she had, and the way she would throw her head back when she laughed, making her drop earrings joggle. She could and did say, by heart, "The Night Before Christmas" and "The Drunk Deacon." Because Ansel knew what he had, Edna would turn up at church on Mother's Day with an orchid corsage. Always.

She would make certain that the church had a float in the Grange Fair Parade if it meant that she herself had to put on a silly hat, sit down in the bed of her son's pickup and pretend to be fishing out the back while a piece of poster board (which she had lettered in her large, clear educator's hand) proclaimed the words of Jesus: "I will make you fishers of men." There is another piece of poster board that we use every year: "Enter to Worship, Depart to Serve."

How to replace her . . . Not possible. But I will say this. I visited the school one afternoon last week, and Bertha Brown, Edna's daughter, was standing in the doorway shepherding kids onto the bus at the end of the day. She used precisely the same motion of her arm that her mother had, a repeated circular gesture as she touched each child's shoulder . . .

Estonia and New Hampshire

About a year and a half ago a letter came to the South Danbury Church, addressed to me, asking if our congregation would like to sponsor one of our members to take part in a Bridges for Peace exchange. Bridges for Peace is a coalition of civic, educational, and church groups working to build peace through understanding by arranging reciprocal visits between Soviet and American citizens.

I've loved Russian literature for a long time—in translation, I quickly add—and in particular the plays and stories of Anton Chekhov. I wanted to go. I asked the church membership if I might represent them on this trip, and everyone said yes, gladly.

I knew little about Estonia, only that it is one of the Baltic Republics. But when I learned that half of the group's time would be spent there, I began to read in earnest about it, and I became aware how much news from that country appears in American newspapers.

In October of 1988 I drove in the dark to the Trailways bus station in Concord on one of those foggy, dewy, delicately melancholy mornings. From Boston's Logan Airport we flew to Kennedy, and when I saw "Aeroflot" in Cyrillic lettering on the plane's fuselage, I knew I'd started something. Then came the long flight to Moscow.

Chekhov loved the city, but the northern cold aggravated his tuberculosis, eventually forcing his move to Yalta, in the Crimea. But when he was fresh out of medical school, he opened his practice in Moscow in the house that is now a museum. There's a simple wooden sign on the door: "Dr. A. P. Chekhov." Shuffling around inside on paper slippers to spare the parquet floors, I saw drafts of his stories and plays, letters, his black, cracking leather doctor's bag. The last thing in the exhibit, his spectacles—*pince-nez*—shocked me as a lock of Keats's hair had once shocked me in Hampstead.

From Moscow we took a night train to Tallinn, the capital of Estonia. At dawn the train began to slow. A sound of tinkling bells came nearer and nearer to our compartment until the steward entered with glasses of strong tea. Though I had read a good deal about the country, the landscape surprised me as we neared the station, for we passed through sandy railroad ravines that looked like ours in Wilmot. Birch trees were shedding their golden leaves in the morning damp, and the small farms had been neatly prepared for winter.

The Tallinn Peace Committee met us with flowers at the station, and put us up in a strikingly modern hotel, a highrise built cooperatively with Finns and Finnish capital. Estonia is so close to Finland, and the Finnish language so similar to Estonian, that many Estonians watch Finnish television. They get to practice their English by watching American shows: *Little House on the Prairie* is a big favorite.

Then came a week of visits to schools, factories, churches, hospitals. We encountered nothing but spontaneous kindness everywhere. And planned kindness, for the Estonians are incorrigibly kind.

Once I got home, I began to think about bringing Estonian visitors to South Danbury. How should we represent ourselves, our community? I wrote some letters, and made some calls, and gradually worked up a schedule that was similar to the Estonian itinerary. And so, on a recent Monday, my friend Mary Lyn Ray and I drove to Pelham to pick up Raivo Jarvi and Toivo Pilli, an illustrator of children's books, and a Baptist minister.

The next morning we visited the Danbury School, and in the afternoon, the Alexandria School—one room, and smaller, Raivo said, than any he had ever seen. Raivo does a television show for kids in Estonia. He draws for them and talks—how to put it—about life. He does an imitation of the Smurfs, saying, "I *hate* tables without sweeties!"

Speaking of sweeties, how Raivo loved the fresh fruit I keep in a big bowl on the dining-room table. He couldn't get enough. He's big, and athletic, and at home he couldn't buy such fruit at any price—it's simply not available. And while we're on the subject of sweeties and shortages, Raivo's mother is diabetic. She must forgo her beloved sweeties for another reason, and there are times when she can't get insulin to keep her disease under control. It's not that the USSR doesn't have enough medication for its citizens, Raivo said, but that the distribution of goods is carried out unfairly, Estonian products supplying Moscow to the detriment of Estonia.

On our tour of Concord Hospital Raivo drew a big raccoon for a sick child in Pediatrics while Toivo prayed quietly in the doorway. And so the five days of our visit flew past. . . .

Gary Johnson, Director of Quality at Freudenberg IPC in Bristol, gave us a tour of the plant where so many of our neighbors have jobs making gaskets of all kinds for private industry and the government. We left with not one, but five or six gifts each, and driving out past the factory entrance we saw the sign we had missed on the way in: "US—USSR Bridges for Peace. Welcome Toivo Pilli and Raivo Jarvi." The company had even tried to locate an Estonian flag to make our visitors feel at home. Of course we hopped out of the car and took pictures of our blond young men smiling broadly.

We wandered in the streets of Bristol for a while. Mary Lyn and I wanted our friends to see the five-and-ten there, a classic. As it happened, I found some small flags with the New Hampshire state seal on them, which I bought when Raivo and Toivo weren't looking. Then we walked up the hill to the Federated Church to a tea in honor of our citizen diplomats. We sat in a circle as they explained the situation at home, the rapidly accelerating pace of *perestroika*.

Estonia was an independent nation from 1920 to 1940, when Stalin annexed the area into the USSR and collectivized the rich farms. But many Estonians remember a time when they went their own way. Our visitors think of themselves as Estonians, not as Russians, and they look forward to a more independent status. Estonian has just been made the official language, displacing Russian. The next big hurdle they see is getting their own currency. When someone expressed concern for their safety Raivo said, "We won't give them any reason to use force."

Mary Lyn made the point that we are in danger of becoming anti-Soviet out of feeling for the Estonians, and that becoming anti-Soviet is not what Bridges for Peace is all about.

Another day Bud Thompson took us through the Shaker Village in Canterbury, giving in one morning a trenchant view of the Shaker experiment in communal living, and at noon, a Shaker meal.

At last it was Friday night, our last evening together at the Church potluck supper. I had been hoarding this occasion the way some people collect fireworks all year for one hour's happiness in July. The crowd was big, the food was bounteous American rural New England, which is to say casseroles with Ritz crackers on top, and Jell-O salads, and homemade pies. Afterward, our guests' talk about their country was frank and detailed. A few years ago it might have landed them in jail, but then even a year ago neither of them would have been granted a visa to travel to the United States: Toivo and Raivo are not Communist Party members.

We had borrowed the trio—The Old Plow—from Shaker Village for the evening, and they were marvelous with songs like "Stay on the farm, boys, stay on the farm . . ." Then we all sang "God Be with You 'Til We Meet Again," and Toivo gave a benediction that grew and grew as we listened, a deeply felt blessing.

It was painful to let Raivo and Toivo go the next afternoon in Newport, where we turned them over to their Vermont hosts. They would be five days in Vermont, and then back to New York briefly before leaving for Moscow.

I asked them where they would land in the USSR, thinking that

Leningrad would be closer to Estonia than Moscow. "You can only enter the country through Moscow. It is a law." They were going back to their accustomed long lines for food, restrictions, small enervating irritations.

Raivo was married just a week before he left for America. He had made seven attempts to get a visa for an American trip, and at last the Russian government had relented. So he had left his bride, bringing with him a single bottle of champagne. There had been no champagne at the wedding. He could get only the one bottle, which we opened on our last evening together. It was marvelous, thick, and not terribly dry, tasting a little like mead—like honey and sunshine in a bottle.

The Mailbox

Our mailing address is R.D., Danbury, N.H. 03230, even though we live in Wilmot. People here used to go the other way to get their mail, to Henry Powers's store in West Andover, but that was when mail came in as many as four times a day at the train station and there was no rural delivery here at all. Danbury did have mail delivery, beginning in 1903, and sometime in the 1950s this house became part of the Danbury route.

Usually we let Bruce Dill bring our mail to the large, somewhat battered mailbox on Route 4. (Its door is askew from being bashed by the town plow.) Occasionally, though, we expect something so enticing that one of us drives to intercept the mail before Bruce leaves on his rounds.

Our brick-and-stone post office is as homely as Larry Bird, and just as indispensable. Mail delivery isn't half of it. "If there's trouble anywhere . . ." goes the old hymn. All disasters and formidable occasions, personal or civic, register on the P.O. bulletin board. If there's been a fire, there will be a note saying where to take clothes and household items; if an animal is missing or if there are free kittens, a number to call; if someone has died, an envelope for memorial contributions. Announcements of Grange suppers, raffles for the fire department, rabies clinics—they all go up on the board.

When we have finished with our magazines and seed catalogs, we take them down to the P.O. to add to the communal pile in the lobby. (It doesn't seem right to call it a lobby—it's too small.) I've hesitated to take back issues of *Soviet Life*. I don't want to alarm anybody.

During the warm months our postmaster, Pat Moran, plants and attends pinwheel petunias in the raised bed by the door, redeeming the building's looks a little. Inside, geraniums bloom on the windowsill. They blossom all winter, through nights when it's 35 degrees below zero and mornings when the car shrieks if you try to start it.

On days when I don't drive to the P.O., I'm glad to hear the tires of Mr. Dill's gray station wagon slow down as he approaches our box, then the crunch of gravel, then the sound of the box opening and closing. Bruce is the bringer of possibilities—he bringeth and he taketh.

He's quite calm about it, but we stop mid-sentence whenever he arrives. We might be working or catnapping, talking on the phone or having lunch, but one of us bolts for the box. Usually my husband gets there first. His legs are longer, and his chair is closer to the door.

Once for my birthday he gave me a gadget that played Beethoven's "Für Elise" every time someone opened the mailbox, but it stopped working after a violent thunderstorm. Now it plays only if the power falters, and has come to mean, "Reset the digital clocks." We'll have to replace it with one that works, and plays the "Ode to Joy."

Two writers generate a lot of outgoing mail. Surely we are among the P.O.'s best customers for stamps, postcards and air-letter forms. Once in a while the U.S. government issues a stamp with a poet on it—Emily Dickinson, T. S. Eliot, Robert Frost—and we really stock up. Much of my personal correspondence goes out on postcards. For fifteen cents you get not only the postage but the card as well. You have to be taciturn or have small handwriting.

One of the nicest things Mr. Dill does for us every year (and in years before him, Bert Hillsgrove) is to lug our annual bushel of Florida oranges to the door. All the better if it is snowing at that very moment: When I lift the lid, the oranges seem to exude heat and light along with their sharply pleasant scent.

Whenever I can't contain myself and go in early to get the mail,

I'm amazed by the number of people who have P.O. boxes, who pull briskly into the parking lot, leave their motors running and unlock the small brass doors inside with an economy of motion that comes only of long practice. Why can't they wait for Mr. Dill? I thought only writers cared so much about the mail.

Season of Change and Loss

All Saints' and All Souls' have circled around again: All Saints', a cele-
bration of the lives of the Christian saints and martyrs, and All Souls',
a remembrance of the souls of ordinary believers through all time.

Maybe your faith does not mark these days, or maybe you belong
to no religious persuasion, or your persuasion is to have no persua-
sion, but you recognize the season "When yellow leaves, or none, or
few, do hang/Upon those boughs which shake against the cold,/Bare
ruin'd choirs, where late the sweet birds sang."

You may already have left the hose to drain down some sloping
place in the yard, planted a few bulbs, raked a few leaves. Possibly
you've pulled down the winter sashes on the storm windows and no-
ticed the increasingly strident calling of crickets from the grass. The
autumn sun can't dry the dew from the lawn, even on the brightest af-
ternoon. The grass is lush, spendthrift, doomed.

A few small, unharvested green tomatoes dangle from blackened
plants, having frozen modestly in their pots on the porch. The smell
of them is pungent, close to the smell of edible food but a little off.
Rainwater in the ashtray on the garden table freezes by night and
thaws again by day.

Acorns drop from the oaks with a sound like rain, acorns this year
small but plentiful. They've come down without their tops so that we
miss the childish pleasure of whistling on their caps. Geese fly over in
sweet disorder, controlled chaos, one leader pulling the string for a
while, then another emerging to take the leader's place. The dog looks
up to see where the commotion is coming from.

Good-bye to flesh. Turtlenecks and woolens come out of drawers and garment bags smelling of naphthalene, and the resumption of sober activities in public places, and love in a cold climate. Good-bye to getting the paper barefoot, or nipping out to the kitchen garden for a handful of basil or chervil. The basket on top of the fridge fills with odd hats and gloves, and our sandals withdraw discreetly to the back of the closet.

Little deaths. Somewhere in the psyche all these changes and losses register as death. What shall we do against it? One might bake a pie, as Joyce Maynard has been doing all summer against the big kind of death—the death of her mother. "Comfort me with apples . . ." Just now there are many kinds: Macouns, Spartans, Gravensteins, Empires, Paula Reds, Baldwins, Northern Spies. It is a fine thing to build a pie, a bulwark against autumnal entropy.

Another defense against reality is to confront it—to admit the pervasiveness of change and loss and replacement. We are in fact like the grass that flourishes and withers, just as the psalmist says. Gardening teaches this lesson over and over, but some of us are slow to learn. We can only acknowledge the mystery, and go on planting burgundy lilies.

Walking. Something else to do besides baking pies and planting bulbs. The bugs are gone, and the deer hunt hasn't started in earnest. We're free to notice the multitude of drying vines and grasses, mushrooms and puffballs, like the one that's growing faster than a shopping mall in the backyard. The dog's afraid of it.

Leaves come down around us, and the profile of the land emerges again, coming clear as a thought. Now we see ledges and stone walls that had been obscured by ferns and brush all summer. Now we see architecture; some of us see bones.

At twilight the sedges are purple, and, as if to compensate for the loss of day, the sunsets become more resplendent than ever. These are the skies through which, my Methodist grandmother used to tell me,

Jesus will come a second time into the world, trailing clouds of glory, to judge the quick and the dead.

Certainly diminishing light contributes to our sense of loss. Not for nothing that Christmas and Chanukah—celebrations of light's triumph over darkness—come when the sky is indigo by 4:30. Even before the stores have finished touting Halloween—All Hallows' Eve is a variant name for All Saints'—I begin to string sets of small white lights on the larger houseplants in the parlor.

No more mowing after supper in the buttery light. We come inside, where the evenings are long and silent. Baseball is dead; even Commissioner Giamatti is dead. There are books, the consolations of philosophy. There's one last cricket in the window well, sounding half-convinced, and a spider I brought in unintentionally with the geraniums, who lives in the general area of the sink.

My plan is to live like the bears: to turn the compost a few more times, prowl around a little longer and then go to sleep until the white-throated sparrow, with its coarse and cheerful song, calls me out of the dark.

Every Year the Light

Each year at the South Danbury Church for the four Sundays preceding Christmas, we light a candle in the Advent wreath, until, on the Sunday of Christmas week, all of them are lit—one each Sunday and one for good measure, the Christ candle.

During Advent the Sunday School, with mixed anticipation and dread, prepares a program to be given a few nights before Christmas. The students speak pieces from memory, and put on a tableau of the Nativity. Every year the wise men's flannel bathrobes and foil crowns, the shepherds' staves, the plywood creche bristling with hay, the tinsel halos, pillowcase burnooses, and foil wings come down the attic ladder in the vestibule.

Not *Oedipus Rex,* not *Hamlet,* not *The Cherry Orchard* played by the finest players could be more moving than the children of South Danbury dressed as Mary and Joseph and kneeling over a doll from Sears.

Something ancient and well-loved transpires before our eyes. "And a little child shall lead them." Heedless power and pride threaten our world, but with a child, a baby, we begin again, in innocence. The hairs on the back of my neck bristle.

What happens in the pageant is beyond personality. Different children fill the roles over the years, but the play goes on, renewing itself like a compost infinitely rich and life-giving.

Edna Powers, who often wrote the verses for the recitations, and always stood in the shadows ready to prompt a child struck dumb with shyness, died at Eastertime. We will miss her calm presence, her dangling, glinting crystal earrings, her deep pleasure in the proceed-

88

ings. With much difficulty we admit that she is gone from us, but the play tells us that "the light shines in the darkness, and the darkness has not overcome it."

Every year, after the manger scene, Edna's son, Peter Powers, bursts in dressed as Santa, changing the mood entirely, to distribute the presents under the tree, his appearance preceded by the sound of harness bells in the cold air, something else that raises my hackles.

In former times the families of South Danbury didn't have Christmas trees at home. The one at church did for all, and under it the little girls who grew up in our house in the early part of this century found dolls with bisque heads and eyes that moved, maybe new mittens, a book, possibly an orange—pungent, heavy and cool to touch.

Even now the presents under the Church tree tend to be simple. No one gets Nintendo, in which the gun is the answer to everything. No one gets a PC. We have yet to see our first toy automatic assault rifle, though I suppose there's a first time even for that. But for now it's tins of homemade cookies, handmade aprons, boot socks, picture puzzles, and embroidered tea towels.

So we light a new candle each week, and we wait, and meanwhile where are our hearts and minds as we go about our business in the Advent season? We stand in line, ill-tempered and anxious, to ply our Visa cards and empty our checkbooks. More money, more love. We're so loving we can hardly pay our bills. We forget, while we're sighing, shifting our weight from haunch to haunch, and contemplating apostasy to the next register, that the kingdom of God is within us.

Every year I swear I won't enter the fracas, and every year I do enter it: I am the fracas. Like Saint Paul (in this, only, I think we are alike), the thing I would not do is the very thing I do. If I am made of the same stuff as the stars, why am I perturbed not to find a parking place near the bookstore, and why do I watch with dismay as the person ahead of me makes off with the shapeliest tree?

Have you noticed that Advent calendars in the stores have more and more to do with Santa's workshop and less and less to do with Mary's confinement? I've even seen scratch-and-sniff calendars, and calendars with a chocolate wafer behind each door.

Our church sends baskets to shut-ins at Christmas, and sometimes it falls to me to shop for such things as ginger ale, oranges, ribbon candy, little packets of Kleenex, and the like. I brace myself for this outing among the wide-aisled grocery stores of Concord as if I were going into battle. I want to get as much as I can, for as little as possible, as fast as I can, forgetting that the real gifts live in the air.

My soul needs the steadily growing joy of Advent and the church pageant to quiet itself, to stop the thrashing. Another important antidote to the fumes of the marketplace is the Christmas Eve candlelight service at the Wilmot Center Church, led by Dr. Jack Jensen, who is our pastor as well as Wilmot Center's. Jack also teaches religion and philosophy at Colby-Sawyer College in New London. I've seen him in academic and in pastoral robes—one scarlet, the other blue.

At the Christmas Eve service we sing carols, and Jack reads once again an account of the first Christmas. How thrilling those words are when we really hear them—like a familiar, much-loved face looked at with concentration: "Behold a virgin shall be with child, and shall bring forth a son, and they shall call his name Emmanuel, God with us."

At the end of the service someone turns out the lights, and we remain in darkness for several moments. Then Judy Walker lights one candle, and with that flame she turns to the person next to her, lighting that candle, and so the light grows to fill the sanctuary. Then we sing "Silent Night," and go home.

Whatever Advent means for us as individuals—and maybe it means nothing to you because your faith takes you elsewhere, or because you have no faith, and are not looking to have it—Advent means light in a dark time. And for Christians it means the hope of starting over as the Christ child's life meant starting over in a new covenant with God.

The Five-and-Dime

A few weeks back, in one of the *Monitor's* year-end retrospective pieces, I saw a picture of Woolworth's on Concord's Main Street, which closed in 1984, the last of the city's four dime stores to surrender to the pressures of the upscale. My hairdresser, who grew up in Pembroke, tells me that the macaroni and cheese at Woolworth's was very fine. I never had a meal there, but I used to browse contentedly among its fifty-thousand things, while the wooden floor creaked under my feet.

What have we done to our real dime stores? They've gone the way of local bakeries and indigenous breweries. Somehow Kmart seems antiseptic. I miss the smell of hot grease, of nuts roasting; the twitterings of parakeets and lovebirds; the steamy windows; the bubbling abundance of the fish tank, with its solitary deep-sea diver wandering over the blue gravel on the tank's bottom; the glass cases full of candy, and the woman in the white uniform who weighed the candy out and handed it over in a white paper bag. When you were little she handed it over and down and accepted your money with an amusement that puzzled you. For Proust's hero it was the smell and taste of a madeleine dunked in a cup of lime-flower tea that summoned up the remembrance of things past. For me it's the smells and sounds of a five-and-dime.

I've found, in my ramblings, a few remaining glorious dime stores, where you can still get cedar wall plaques with the Ten Commandments on them, and cotton Peds, and Boston Baked Beans, the candy for adults, by the pound. Consider searching them out the next time you feel the need for an excursion.

Bristol's five-and-dime is right around the corner from the Civil War monument. There I once saw a toaster shaped like a pup tent, with side doors that let down so you could turn the toast over and keep an eye on things. It wasn't electric—you put the contraption over a stove burner.

The last time I visited Bristol the toaster was no longer there, but I consoled myself with oil cloth by the yard, baby clothes, sparklers, butter dishes, bayberry candles, and heart-shaped doilies. Recently the store did away with its creaking wooden floor, disturbing the ethos with the silence of carpeting.

Then there is Newberry's in Franklin. Prime shopping time there is in August, when the store is full of back-to-school merchandise. This time of year the aisles are somewhat bare—I'd guess that's so the store won't have to pay tax on a huge inventory. Nonetheless you may find among the shelves blue canvas satchels with red leather straps, photo albums with birch trees on the cover, big bags of cheap candy, an array of women's underwear that caters to the Junoesque and the anorexic, but not much in between, three-corner pillows for reading in bed, plastic swan planters, and the only kind of nail polish my mother-in-law will use.

White River Junction, Vermont, still has a real dime store—Newberry's again—just down from the Hotel Coolidge: plastic flamingoes for your lawn, cheerleader sets consisting of baton and pompoms, and the kind of apron the older women still wear at church-fair suppers. You put your arms through holes to get them on.

At Newberry's in Portsmouth, a three-level affair, you can even have your hair done. The Franklin Newberry's used to have a basement. Several years ago it was closed—an ill omen, I feared. But Housewares regrouped on the first floor, and the store seems to be thriving.

The trouble with New London is that it has no dime store.

Ashland's dime store, like Bristol's, appears to be an independent.

The flaking gilt wooden sign says: W.M. Bailey, 5¢–$1.00. William Maxwell, one of our finest contemporary novelists, wrote a book called *Time Will Darken It,* words that always come to me when I wander in Bailey's dimly lit interior. You can still get beanbag ashtrays, heavy green melton pants, and jackets for working in the woods (if you try the Eddie Bauer catalog I'm sure you can get just about the same thing for three times as much), penny candy and candy by the pound, and thick, ecru envelopes for paying your bills discreetly.

If you ever find yourself in Charleston, South Carolina, don't miss the dime store on Broad Street. (I hope it survived the hurricane.) I bought an eraser there that is at least eight inches long and three inches wide and emblazoned: FOR BIG MISTAKES. For a pittance I got a pair of earrings that look like gold and blue enamel out of the Tiffany catalog. They're heavy and uncomfortable to wear, so I wear them only briefly, for a grand illusion.

In Rome, at the end of the Via Frattina opposite the Spanish Steps, there is a dime store I plan to revisit soon . . .

It's true that Rich's and Ames's have some of the things I've mentioned, but somehow objects lose their particularity in the larger setting, where huge banks of fluorescent lights make all the colors funny, and lost kids are truly lost, and there is never anyone around to answer questions. And of course half the fun of real dime stores, aside from their dedicated *thinginess,* is that the stuff is really cheap. When the purple and black underpants from the People's Republic of China don't fit, you haven't lost much except *amour-propre.*

We live, increasingly, in a world of Wonder bread and Bud Light. The authentic dime store still exists, but marginally. Support your local, or your nearest-to-local, or you may have nowhere to turn for cornucopia decals for your breadbox, or David and Goliath plastic placemats.

A Gardener of the True Vine

Recently the *Monitor* announced Jack Jensen's death. Jack was professor of philosophy and religion at Colby-Sawyer College, minister of the Wilmot Center and South Danbury Congregational churches and a dear friend.

Jack used to say that the Church is the Body of Christ. As such it is indestructible, but just now the body is sore. All of Jack's parishioners are grieving; I can speak best, I suppose, for myself.

When my husband and I moved to Wilmot fifteen years ago, Jack had already been preaching at South Danbury for three years. Except for weddings and funerals, I hadn't been in church since my adolescence, when I'd announced to my parents that I wanted to stop attending Ann Arbor's First Methodist Church because "you can't be an intellectual and a Christian." (Big news, certainly, for Thomas Aquinas, Paul Tillich, Martin Luther, Soren Kierkegaard, and others.)

I had put my gold and blue Methodist Youth Fellowship pin in the bottom of my jewelry box, where I would never see it. Nature and beauty would be my god, and I would be a good person without benefit of the sacraments, just by trying.

So when my husband suggested we go to the South Danbury Church that Sunday in July 1975, I was flabbergasted. We had passed the Sundays of our early married life in Ann Arbor recovering from English Department parties and perhaps playing a little tennis at the Racquet Club.

Don put on a jacket and tie, I put on a skirt, and we drove the three miles to the South Danbury Church. We sat in the back pew, on the right, behind Don's cousin Edna Powers and her husband Ansel, their daughter Bertha and Bertha's husband and children. It turns out we were sitting where Don's ancestors have been sitting since the church was incorporated in 1867.

Jack entered the sanctuary carrying his robe and stole over his arm, having driven the back road from Wilmot Center, where he had preached the 9:30 service. He swung his vestments over his shoulders and headed for the pulpit, a handsome man in the power of early middle age.

The sermon was elegantly shaped and intellectually convincing. What is more, it made reference to the German poet Rainer Maria Rilke. I wouldn't mind hearing this man again, I thought. The cousins and neighbors were pleased to see us and encouraged us to come again.

It's one thing to have faith as a child; one professes belief at least partly out of obedience. Choosing to have a spiritual life as an adult is altogether different. I listened to Jack's sermons week after week, discovering to my astonishment that my soul had been starving. He had what I needed, and I could accept it from him because I respected his mind and his training.

I began to get a feeling for the church year—the way it overlies the biological year, the passing of the seasons. Jack was the shepherd of his sheep, and he slipped his crook around my neck so gently that I was part of the South Danbury fold before I knew what had happened.

I asked him what I should read. He told me to start with Mark's Gospel, using William Barclay's commentary. Not long after, a few members of the Wilmot Center Church began a Bible study group, and we joined them, concentrating on the Prophets, taking months over Isaiah.

Jack turned me toward the women mystics—Saint Teresa, Julian of Norwich, Simone Weil. I read, at his suggestion, the *Confessions* of Saint Augustine, *The Cloud of Unknowing* and *The Imitation of Christ*. One by one he gave his treasures to me.

We talked. . . . This winter, while Jack was so ill, he tried to help me overcome my discomfort with Saint Paul's misogyny in the Epistles. While in Italy in February, my husband and I went to the Mamertine Prison in Rome, where Paul was imprisoned, and to the Abbey of the Three Fountains, where Paul was beheaded—for our friend, for Jack; we came back bearing pictures.

Jack gave me a spiritual life—it's that simple. Over the years my poetry changed to reflect my awakening. Life changed profoundly. I began to feel grateful for things that I had always taken for granted. I began to feel a personal connection to the figure of Christ, God's second self, surely, but also a man who wept to find Lazarus dead, a man with a temper, a man who fell down in the garden in grief and fear.

Thanks to Jack, I became a Hospice volunteer, because I felt for the first time that I must serve, something that had never occurred to me before. Nine years later, I still volunteer for Hospice of the Kearsarge Valley, and through me, Jack has touched some lives that he never knew about.

I'm only one of his agents. If you think that he served two churches for eighteen years, and Colby-Sawyer for thirty, you might have some idea how this man's life resonated and ramified in our corner of the world. I just reminded myself, by looking it up, that "ramified" means "to divide into branch-like parts, to branch out." Jack was a gardener of the true vine.

How he loved a good joke, and he often began his morning in the pulpit by telling one. He loved the sun. He loved to sing, and his strong voice lasted through two sermons and six hymns every Sunday. He loved plants and flowers. An aspidistra that he gave me years ago, for my thirtieth birthday, has just put up seven new leaves after its winter sleep, as if in answer to the desolation we feel. Perennials from my garden are stirring now in his garden.

Jack was a fine amateur photographer, and he recorded wonderfully the trips he and Jo took to Greece, which was his spiritual home.

I remember with particular delight some slides of wildflowers on a hill outside Athens. There is Jo, bronze from the Mediterranean sun, sitting in a thicket of flowering wild thyme. You can practically hear the bees.

Jack never stopped giving. Thirty-six hours before his death he was planning for classes. He loved his friends; he radiated love. The sicker he got, the more radiant he became. The evening before he died he roused himself, summoned what was left of his vision, looked at his visitors, and smiled broadly, nothing held back, with a joy untouched by fear.

The Body of Christ, the Church, is organic and alive. It has lost an arm, but, like a starfish, it will grow a new one. Jack would be moved by our grief, I know, but he would repeat, as he often did, his personal variation on a well-known verse: "This is a day that the Lord has made. We will rejoice and *get on with it.*"

Summer Comes Alive

This morning the sound of a trumpet playing reveille penetrates the fog, echoing up the hills. It comes from the camp loudspeaker on the far side of Eagle Pond, and it means that the staff, at least, has returned to Camps Kenwood and Evergreen.

My husband's grandmother, who lived in this house for 93 of her 97 years, loved hearing reveille in the morning and taps at night. When we first moved here, the sound annoyed me, but I have come to love it, too. Summer is official on the first morning those notes come floating over the field.

Sometime in the next few days a convoy of silver-and-red Concord Trailways buses—majestic, larger than life—will turn down the dusty pond road, just clearing the bridge railing. Soon we'll hear children's voices, dogs barking, and the slamming of cabin screen doors.

Everything has been made ready. The docks and floats are back in the water, the cabins scrubbed, the tennis nets pulled tight and straight, the bases and baselines put down on the ballfields. Yesterday I saw a Weeks Dairy truck turn down the pond road, and I know we are getting close. Camp re-animates before us, like a flower opening—reliably, even ineluctably.

This morning on our walk, the dog and I encountered one of the counselors on his constitutional. He must be from Boston: his arms and legs were bare. He'll be scratching fly bites for some days to come unless he was loaded up with Cutter's. There's another counselor—if she's here this year—who runs every day, late in the afternoon, no matter how hot it gets, and turns an alarming shade of red. She doesn't jog, she *runs,* and she has the taut physique of a person who habitually stretches her limits.

When the wind is right we hear announcements and odd bits of music on this side of the pond. The voice that says, mid-afternoon, "Milk and cookie time . . ." is so enticing that I too long for a cold glass of milk and a ginger cookie. We also hear John Philip Sousa marches (moving music, I suppose, for propelling children from one activity to another), the injunction to write home and, on rainy days, "Raindrops Keep Falling on My Head."

Another characteristic camp noise comes from the waterskiing in-struction—the sound of the boat circling and circling the pond, and words of warning or encouragement spoken through a bullhorn: "Bend your knees! Relax!"

The boys take their instruction in the morning, before the sun is high and warm, the girls in the heat of afternoon. Waterskiing is the only camp activity that troubles me a little: I suspect that the com-motion keeps water birds from nesting. Well, the campers serve as our water birds—our bright, evanescent companions.

Midsummer brings Parents' Weekend, and a succession of Peu-geots, BMWs and Mercedes passes over the bridge. It signals, like the All-Star break in baseball, that the warm nights and dewy flowers are passing, along with strawberries, church fairs, and bathing suits dry-ing on the porch. Local restaurants fill with briefly reunited families, curious parents, and stonewalling sons and daughters:

"Do you like camp?"

"Sure."

"What do you do all day?"

"Oh, different stuff."

Sometimes kids from neighboring camps come here for swim-ming meets. Then we hear loud cheers and chanting. Sometimes our campers go off for the day to neighboring camps, and when they do, the valley is so quiet that from our swimming place on the pond we can hear someone who has stayed behind, practicing on the dining-room piano, veering off into a mistake over and over at the same spot in the Scarlatti sonata. This snag, for some reason, makes me sad.

Sad, too, the day when the big buses reappear, raising dust on the pond road, severing the passionate adolescent friendships of a summer. While everyone's intentions are good, and there are vows of faithfulness, many of the kids have seen each other for the last time. When they get home, heavy with each other's secrets, their mothers will take them shopping for clothes and books, and another life will obtain.

By dusk that August day the docks will have been taken up, the canoes shedded for the winter, everything dismantled, like a circus leaving town. Reveille and taps will continue to sound for a few days, then the food deliveries will cease, and then we'll hear nothing, except, perhaps, the sound of a fish jumping and falling back into the pond.

The water itself grows still, turning a silver-black color, and it reflects the first crimson flare of the swamp maples, and birch leaves changing from green to gold.

But for now we have reveille, fresh milk, and the pleasures of imminence.

The Physics of Long Sticks

We have a ginger-and-white dog named Gus, short for Augustus. (My husband had been reading Roman history when Gus nosed his way into our lives.)

Gus is a moggy, a pet of uncertain parentage, who joined our household five years ago, after bouncing around from pillar to post for the first year or so of his life. There's surely some border collie in him—he has a small collie build, and he shows some herding instinct, nipping at my heels whenever I pull my feet up into bed. There may be some spaniel in him, for he wears white spats, and spots on his spats, along with feathers between his toes. And there is certainly some golden retriever in him, for he never comes home from our outings without a stick in his mouth.

Gus feels unfulfilled without a stick—like a superfluous person. Often I find one for him (he finds his own if I'm preoccupied) on our daily walk up New Canada Road, a narrow gravel lane that goes up Ragged Mountain. Gus and I are on waving terms with quite a few commuting neighbors—nurses, builders, real-estate brokers—since we're all up and out before seven. They laugh at the dog as he labors with a branch five feet long, or longer, chomping it smack in the middle and trotting with his white plumed tail held high, his ears erect. We won't have to send him to MIT when he grows up; he's already figured out the physics of long sticks.

Shorter sticks he grasps at one end, making him look like the flutist Jean Pierre Rampal. Occasionally his totem breaks, leaving only a stub in his mouth, and then he resembles the Boston Celtic eminence Red Auerbach with his omnipresent cigar.

Gus and I set out in all weathers—extreme cold, driving rain, whatever nature proffers. The only thing he minds is wind: wind gives him the *hoo-ha's*. We slip and slide, we get muddy, we slap at flies, we witness the turning of the trees, our breath blooms white in front of us, but we love to start the day by seeing the moon set over Eagle Pond, by overhearing the guttural domestic murmurs of a sleepy crow.

One recent morning Gus took off into the woods after an animal, a common occurrence. I heard nails on bark as the animal skittered up a tree—noisier than usual. It must be a coon, I thought; at least it's something bigger than a squirrel. I called the dog; he didn't come. Called again. No Gus.

I stepped into the woods to look for him when halfway up the nearest oak, I saw a bear cub, black, with huge ears flopping like rabbit ears. I was thrilled until I realized that if mama bear was anywhere about, Gus and I were in trouble.

When a neighbor told me, several days later, that he had seen a large black bear near the bottom of New Canada Road, I boasted of our adventure. "If it ever happens again," he told me, "you run for home. Leave the dog if you have to, but *run*. You're more important than the dog."

I don't know. . . . Gus is an inspiration and a model of behavior for our household. He's been the subject of doggerel—appropriately— and even of rhapsodic prose. He's incapable of bitterness or cynicism. He's a master at stating his needs: "Feed me. Let me out."

Whenever he feels insecure, this dog engages in the transportation of shoes. He rarely chews them; he simply changes their venue and drops them. When company comes, when we begin packing for a trip, when the red-haired granddaughters come to visit, a trail of shoes appears between the bedroom and the kitchen door, like the line of breadcrumbs in the fairy tale. "I need love! I need all your attention, and both of your hands!"

Why can't people be more like dogs—more direct, more openly affectionate, less prone to rancor, and inclined, despite the risk of ridicule, to take up longer sticks?

The Honey Wagon

Water draining from the bathroom—from the sink, the toilet, the shower—gurgles deep in the pipes under the kitchen sink. Our septic system is as sluggish as a boa constrictor after consuming a mongoose. The tank hasn't been pumped for years.

I call a septic-system cleaning service in Elkins and get a recording. For several days our machines exchange messages.

Finally, I call a service in Franklin, and that afternoon a spruce, compact man, smelling vehemently of aftershave, backs his truck into the drive, dislodging in the process several stone porch steps and a planting of lemon thyme.

He asks where the tank is buried. I have already lifted flowers from the garden under the kitchen window, where I know he'll have to dig, pulling them out of his way, on a thick blue tarp, into the cool shade of the woodshed. He makes a few stabs in the earth with a long metal rod and finds the tank almost immediately.

This brings to mind a similar event from childhood. My family lived in the country when I was growing up, in an old house on the outskirts of Ann Arbor, and I recall the excitement of a long search for the septic tank, a man piercing the grass in the backyard with a metal bar until we heard the thunk of metal hitting cement.

On a recent visit to Michigan I asked my mother if she could remember the man's name. I thought I remembered my father calling him Friendly Reminder, but my mother recalled that Mr. Friendly was the plumber—who once left us without running water for four days while he took off with his sons to hunt deer.

We couldn't summon up the septic man's name, so we took out

the phone book—five times as thick as the phone book of my childhood—to see if our man should still be listed in the yellow pages. "Jack Sprack," Mother said immediately. "On Carpenter Road in Ypsilanti. Serving the Ann Arbor area since 1948."

I recognized the name's euphony and kept reading the ad in its bold box picturing four trucks, the prosperity of forty years of pumping sewage quite evident. Then, in bold print: "In Our Business a Flush Beats a Full House." No danger of forgetting Mr. Sprack again.

Once Mr. Sprack had located the tank, all those years ago, he backed his truck over the lawn, Mother's sharp intake of breath registering the ruts the tires made in the moist earth. He dug without stopping at a moderate pace until the lid of the tank lay aslant on the grass; he lowered the stout hose into the neck of the tank and began to pump. I wanted to get close enough to look into the tank, but I had a morbid fear of the offal. I'm sure I observed the proceedings from the lowest branch of the box elder tree.

This time, thirty-five years later and six hundred miles eastward, I went inside and paced around the house while the man from Franklin dug a hole the size of a seaman's chest, found the lid, and opened it. When he began to pump, I made myself go out and look into the hole. A gray, putrid, frothing glop coursed into the hose—the residue of *nouvelle cuisine,* of glasses of wine taken with friends. It was our washwater, our blood, sweat, and tears. All is vanity.

A septic tank puts us within smelling distance of fundamental truths of rot and renewal. We are not going to live forever: In the midst of life, death and dissolution abide. Yet life has a way of insuring more life. Sewage sludge has been the preferred bulb food in Holland for years. And what is a compost pile to a gardener but a vegetative septic system? Death and birth make a circle, no beginning, no end. The rankest reality can be redeeming.

Our man from Franklin closed the sandy hole and put a marker in the ground so that the next time he comes he can find the lid right away. It is a nasty shade of green, a disk maybe six inches in diameter, fastened to a long stake. I'll do my best to get violets to grow over it. I should call him again in three to five years, he said.

The stone steps tipped back into place easily. I jumped on them a couple of times to settle them, then pressed the thyme back into the earth. Before I could get out the hose to water it all in, a soft but voluminous rain began—the kind that starts abruptly at full force, and doesn't drift or blow but plummets down, the kind that doesn't just dust the leaves but really waters the ground.

Bulbs Planted in the Fall

Last autumn I couldn't get moving. I needed to call the plumber to fix our moribund water heater. I needed to make an eye appointment but feared it was time for the first pair of bifocals. I'd put off clearing brush from the hill until the cool season, when blackflies are only a noxious memory, and now the time had come, but the Japanese pruning saw remained in its wooden sheath.

Worst of all lapses, I'd neglected to order bulbs for the garden. Every other autumn garden chore consists of dismantling or retiring something, but planting bulbs is assemblage, construction, pure optimism—to put a living thing into ground that will soon be frozen to a depth of four feet, and to expect, reasonably, that new life will rise in April.

I went to the local hardware stores, hoping to find at least a few bulbs sufficiently interesting to throw in—something besides King Alfred daffodils and hot red tulips. Maybe I'm a snob, but I prefer white daffodils, and any color—any color—but scarlet tulips. Red is too violent for spring. Only maple flowers and peony shoots and rhubarb leaves are allowed to be red, and they're a cool red, not harsh.

So naturally I came home glum and bulbless, and sat in the parlor in the failing light, dusk falling earlier every day, and thought what a poor ant I am. I'm married to an ant, thank goodness, but I'm a congenital cricket.

"Night and day I sang," says the cricket to the ant, begging a grain of sustenance from its provident neighbor in La Fontaine's fable. "You sang, did you? Well, you just go on singing," replies the stern formicula.

My husband may be an ant—not so censorious as La Fontaine's—but he hadn't ordered white daffodils either.

❧

In late September a writer friend, Alice Goodman, came up from Brookline for the day. When I met her at the Trailways in Concord, she grasped in one hand her daughter Alberta's hand and in the other a large, white nylon bag that I assumed contained little-girl gear—one of the wild, hand-knit jackets Alice makes for her, toys for the trip, diapers, books.

We jabbered the half hour it takes to get to Wilmot, pointing out to Miss Bertie all the horses and cows along the way, and the dogs—which Bert, at the time, pronounced "dowag."

When we were settled at home with cups of strong coffee, and Bert had plucked herself down with our dowag and cat, Alice unzipped the bag to reveal a hundred flat-cupped white narcissus bulbs, called poet's narcissus, late blooming and fragrant; thirty miniature pale yellow narcissus, a variety called Baby Moon; three dozen lily-flowered tulips, yellow and white, pointed at the tips, the kind that become more beautiful as they open, loose, floppy even, more reckless than most tulips.

I remembered then that Alice said she'd bring up some "extras"—but this was a whole shipment!

She had ordered more bulbs for her Brookline garden than she could possibly fit in, a transgression I have committed more than once in the past. Here she'd come to me like Gabriel presenting his lily: she'd brought a surprise and a responsibility. Now I had to get moving.

Over the next week or so I put everything in the ground, working each afternoon in the cool, limpid air, pausing to look at the mountain, a dark purple at that time of year. Nothing could have been more salutary—digging the sandy loam, savoring its smell against a time when earth has no smell.

Alice says that in her enthusiasm for old roses, she has ordered more bushes from the rosery in Nashua than she knows what to do with. Now I'm a believer; I'm already grubbing out junk trees and wild helianthus so I'll be ready when she comes back with a child who has learned to say "dog" and a bagful of Bourbon roses.

A Day to Loaf

Labor Day weekend is a peculiar time—a hiatus between the ease of late summer and the resumption of more concentrated work. The second crop of hay is in, the garden maintains itself, and we are home from our travels with mountains of sandy laundry. We have finished with summer's concerns but have not yet resigned ourselves to autumn's brisk momentum toward the closing of the year.

The first Monday in September honors, as my 1976 edition of *The American Heritage Dictionary* tells me, the working man. I imagine a stock figure, shirtsleeves rolled up, flexing a well-muscled male arm. The realities of 1991 compel us to add a picture of a woman carrying a briefcase and a bag of takeout Chinese food. In any case, this weekend we honor our workers in the traditional way—by ceasing to work.

Yankees equate work with virtue, an attitude that may derive from the religious convictions of the Pilgrims, who saw labor and prosperity as a sign of God's favor, of election, and a failure to thrive as a sign of damnation. Whether the notion is correct, or fair, is questionable, but Labor Day is our time to loaf without reproof, to suspend our righteous doing and engage in simple being.

The garden sprawls. Zucchinis have become the subject of outlandish jokes. We harvest grand tomatoes—one slice fills a sandwich; we stir endless pots of sauce in our hot kitchens. Crickets chirrup in the long grass, and gladiolas lean as if searching for something between the rows. Goldenrod, the instigator of runny eyes and back-to-school foreboding, nods in the ditches and along the margins of the woods.

Summer resolutions may or may not be fulfilled. Perhaps you

stalled two-thirds of the way through the second volume of *The Remembrance of Things Past;* perhaps you kept plugging, and now you question whether to start volume three. Maybe you lost five pounds by eating summer's fresh fruits and vegetables, and maybe, because of Ben and Jerry's Rainforest Peace Pops, certain waistbands continue to vex. A new deck may or may not enhance the back of the house; the hillside may or may not be clear of brush. Well, today is Labor Day, and we'll just have to be the way we are.

A cookout is mandatory at least once this weekend. Lawn chairs sag and sprinklers whirr; children run squealing through sheets of spray. The dog and cat lie in the deep shade of maples, looking hot and frowzy, harassed by fleas.

This weekend the bored and the pressed for time go shopping, particularly if the weather is rainy. The stores burst like seedpods with clothes in autumnal shades. You have to turn sideways to get down the aisles of double-pleated corduroy pants and Shaker sweaters. I think of the Soviets standing in line outside stores with almost empty shelves, facing a chaotic, cold, and hungry autumn.

Everybody wants the good life. . . . But what is the good life? Fifty kinds of sneakers to choose from, some costing as much as a refrigerator used to cost, or a month's rent? We wax our cars until they gleam, we buy our children the latest baggy jeans for school as if clothes could form good minds, make them successful in work, assure them solid marriages, long health, prosperous retirement.

A fresh dry breeze blows this morning. It makes the grass in the field, getting long again after the last mowing, bend and sway abruptly in broad, silver-green swags. The wind blows on all of us, the harried and the becalmed. Time, and our desires, and our labors move us through our lives, but something else—call it providence or happenstance—also moves us, and this is a mystery which we may consider in idleness on this day of official idleness.

A Garden of My Dreams

The odd greeting card dribbles in. Then they arrive—tax forms and flower catalogs. The tax forms, like the undertaker's statement for services rendered, must come to us all, or to our next of kin.

But the catalogs fall into a different category. They might not have come to us, but they did—serendipity. We can pass our winter nights dreaming of white Russian sunflowers, Kentucky Wonder beans heavy on their poles, bright pink asters with yellow eyes, wisteria drooping from redwood arbors, and banks of fragrant yellow daylilies—all when the thermometer reads −5 and the shutters tug on their hinges in a brutal wind.

Oh, the gardens we construct in our heads on these fierce winter evenings!

First, a lot of brush gets cleared by magic, creating room for a forty-foot border of mixed perennials, vegetables, and old shrub roses. By some miracle the proper amount of sun reaches there each day.

Water! Not to worry. It rains in this place at least two inches every week, always at night, so there's no mildew on the phlox and the gardener never has to come inside on account of the weather. Blackflies are unknown in this Eden. Japanese beetles have never invaded its borders. Pear thrips, fireblight, gypsy moths, rust, blackspot: ditto. Unheard of here.

The Better Girl tomatoes grow almost as big as Beefsteaks, but without their elephantine wrinkles—perfectly smooth and easy to peel, immaculate, and weighing a pound apiece. The snap peas squirt when you pop them open. Zucchinis stay the size of large bananas, delicate, tender-skinned, unlike the canoes of other years.

Old shrub roses with romantic French names suffuse the air with their attar. They clothe the side of the barn with pink and white and vermilion blossoms; they run off their trellises, spill onto the ground. Espaliered apple trees grow heavy with Sops of Wine. Bees murmur in the lavender, hummingbirds dip their long beaks into the ten-foot-high, peach-colored fringed hollyhocks . . .

Where am I? Clearly, I've fallen asleep on the couch with the White Flower Farm catalog open on my chest, as the man in Robert Lowell's poem falls asleep over the *Aeneid.* My husband is watching some violent sport on television while dictating letters. I should get up and fill the humidifier for the night. I should floss my teeth. It seems to me that if I could live without flossing my teeth and fastening my seatbelt, I could be truly happy.

Could we stand it, I wonder, scraping my uppers with the floss; could we stand the perfection of our dreams? Where would the challenge lie? *In not dying from a surfeit of beauty.*

As things are, we have our modest triumphs, our outright failures, and our okay vegetables and flowers. At least there's no poison anywhere, except what we've applied ourselves—a little rotenone on the vegetables, and benomyl to keep blackspot off the peonies and delphinium.

We live in an imperfect world, with imperfect characters to match. Our imperfections should not keep us from dreaming of better things, or even from trying, within our limits, to be better stewards of the soil, and more ardent strivers after beauty and a responsible serenity.

The Mud Will Dry

"How long the winter has lasted," begins a poem I know, "like a Mahler/symphony, or an hour in the dentist's chair." Another, called, "Mud Season," begins: "Here in purgatory, bare ground is visible . . ."

It seems we spend eons in this difficult, gray, moldy-looking place, working out the last of our venial sins—venial being serious but not absolutely killing. I had to look it up in the *Concise Oxford Dictionary of the Christian Church* since I grew up a Methodist, and Methodists were either in or out of Saint Peter's gate, on the bus or off the bus. There was no middle ground. Mud season is my middle ground.

It's too early to rake. The ground is wet, and the grass would come up in clumps along with the leaves, covered with dust, road salt, and sand. It's too early for the tulips to bloom, though they keep piercing the mulch.

Over and over I gather more leaves, dump them on the emerging flowers, and lay hemlock boughs on top to keep everything in place. But the strong spring winds dislodge my efforts; either that, or the tulips want so badly to bloom that they will not be thwarted.

That's the touching thing about plants—they want to grow, to be fruitful. You can plant them upside down, as I once did with dahlia tubers, and they still thrive.

Mud season is a time of waiting. Gardeners wait to garden. Farmers wait to lime and plow. Fishermen and -women wait to fish. Housekeepers wait for the first day they can throw open the doors and windows, shake out the bedding and hang it on the line, wash curtains and dry them outdoors. We need a warm wind to blow through us, to cleanse us, restore us. Instead we have muddy ruts in the roads that soften by day and freeze again by night, and moldy-frowzy grass—buff and gray, and utterly without hope of greening in the cold.

We haven't even reached the stage at our place when the housefly brigades wake up and assemble. Soon they'll do so, chased ineffectually by the dog and cat. Growing up, I knew a dog who would snap flies out of the air, swallowing them in a trice. It horrified and fascinated me. Not for nothing was she called "Bitsy." Our animals pursue but fall short, like carabinieri who don't want to muss their uniforms chasing a bank robber because they have an assignation at noon.

"Act as though you had faith," Isaac Bashevis Singer said. "Faith will come afterward." So I cleared the asparagus bed the other day, finding beneath dirty leaves the bent stalks, which should have been cut down last November, and would have been, had we not been walking the streets of New Delhi and Allahabad. The ground was absolutely, unforgivingly frozen. I sprinkled on some 10-10-10, and gardening for 1992 commenced.

Then I came inside and called to get a permit to burn last year's stalks along with a pile of what we call bamboo. This tall and not unattractive plant invades the hayfield a few more feet each year. It's the cockroach of plants, and will survive the terrors of the Book of Revelation. My fire expert told me to rake the stuff into a pile, cover it with plastic, and, on the first rainy day, to appear at his door for a permit.

After five o'clock I may set fire to the offending vegetation. I speculated on the significance of the timing. It could mean "after the wind dies down." Or it could mean that our firefighters like to do battle at a convenient hour—and who can blame them—after work and before supper. I think I could fight a fire with more gusto after dinner myself.

The bamboo and the poplars encroaching steadily on the fields trouble me, and so do the junipers coming up around the big ledge in the east field. I'd like to keep this place looking the way it did when my husband hayed with his grandfather in the '40s, scythe-mowing the edges and corners, cutting back brush when it's called for. Will my back hold out? "Act as though you had faith . . ."

The Shadows

Even as I write these words it begins—the annual, ineluctable summer storm that smashes the fully open peonies. Peonies always bloom at graduation time—a time of beauty and promise of more beauty, soft air, fecundity; a time of bright-eyed kids, and celebration, the girls in their prom dresses ruffled like peonies, pink and white.

Into this voluptuous time comes the storm with wind and hail, trouble and damage. A bright, outgoing boy suddenly puts a gun to his head and pulls the trigger. Frost says, in his dark poem, "Out, Out": "No more to build on there." For the boy's family, life will never be the same.

At our house this June, the smasher is cancer. My husband is sick again, two and a half years after his first surgery. Just when we were beginning to feel safe and blessed, a routine blood exam pointed to the presence of a tumor. CT scans and ultrasound confirmed what we feared, and we spent the early part of May in Hanover. When we entered Taj Med, the trees were leafless; when we came home, the yard was shady.

We had been back ten days when the call came that Don's mother was in Yale New Haven Hospital with a heart attack, having been resuscitated that morning. We pulled ourselves together and went down to Connecticut when she was discharged from the hospital. We stayed eight days, filling her freezer with small packets of pleasing food, and satisfying ourselves that the VNA would take good care of her. We came home just in time for Don's first chemotherapy treatment. And that's when I had the accident with the lawn mower, but that's a horse of a different color . . .

The luckiest, sunniest life invariably includes tragedy, if I do not overstate these matters by calling them tragic. To lose your health, your strength, your ability to work, and to take pleasure in life—that is tragedy. It's no less tragic because it happens to everybody.

It is as the psalmist said, we are like the grass. That's both comforting and upsetting. We are like the peonies, flowering and fading, and there is nothing for it except faith or gritty resignation. We're all in it together, but we don't have to like it. We can't vote death and destruction out of office, and the mysteries are unimpeachable.

Recently I sat at dinner with a man who struck me as energetic and creative, generous to his community, involved in many undertakings. How could there be trouble in that life? I mentioned my husband's illness (we were undergoing an awards ceremony, and there was lots of time to talk), and suddenly he divulged that he had had four operations for cancer, mutilating ones and reconstructive ones. He understood every nuance of our shaken, enfeebled state as I described it. He spoke of the love and support of friends who have the same disease, who have undergone the same helpless turning-themselves-over in order to get done what needed to be done.

You gather all your trust, and you walk into a building where people put you to sleep, cut you open, plunge around in your guts, take out two-thirds of your liver, thrust a respirator down your throat and pull it out again, and then after ten days pull out the bloody drains and send you home, staggered by what has happened to your body, and your plans, and your day-to-day life, which you were so much in the habit of taking as a *given.*

The man I met at dinner is well. He stays well, lives with more awareness of the small blessings of the day, the simple contentment of family life when it is harmonious. This is what we are trying to do at our house: simplify, appreciate, stay close, be kind, tell the truth, work as we are able, rest. We're keeping to ourselves, reading out loud, going to bed early. We make jokes about putting up a Cyclone fence.

Tonight before the storm I went out with the kitchen shears and a basket. I cut every full-open peony in sight, quantities that I would never permit myself under other circumstances. I knew the rain would shatter the flowers, break their stems so that their luxurious forms and perfumes would be lost for the year. Pick them, something told me, pick them and fill the house, and we'll put our faces into them and inhale, and see the ants crawl on them, and leave the ants alone because life is precious and ought not to be crushed.

We are getting an education this summer, in the humanities, I would say—in love despite fear, in the amazing resilience of the human body. And daily we grow in the determination to cast off trouble like a garment in the heat and keep going, keep living, and living abundantly, with more awareness of each moment and more joy.

Dreams of Math

With trepidation I've glanced over the school-bus schedules in the *Monitor* these last few days. Something in me, and I suspect in many of us, still thinks that *they* are going to appear from nowhere to make me go shopping with Mother for books and pencils, then to force me back into the classroom.

The same strange forces robbed me of countless hours wasted on dusty school buses. How well I remember standing in the September morning fog, waiting for the yellow bulk of the school bus to appear out of white air. We could hear the bus long before the twin blinking lights rose to the top of Foster Road and the door swung open.

Though I'm twenty-five years and almost a thousand miles away from my public education, I still dream that I'm lost in the hallways of a school, looking for a locker, which, once found, I cannot open because I have forgotten the combination. Everybody must endure these nightmares about being late, lost, unprepared, and altogether lacking the "pitch and merit" of a successful seventh grader.

How many times have I dreamt that the season for final exams has come, and I go dutifully from room to room taking my tests. But what's this? It seems I have a test in physics, a class in which I have forgotten I was enrolled, and which I have neglected to attend all semester. It is the spring term of my senior year.

Like Keats's sufferer in "La Belle Dame Sans Merci," I awaken "on the cold hillside." My heart races as I begin to plead my case. It's no good—I can't fill a physics blue book with poetry.

Trouble, trouble. Why is there no happy moment in these dreams of school? I guess it's because to be in school was to be anxious, at least for me. I felt liable for the things I didn't know. I must have thought I should be like the last polymath, who lived in the eighteenth century.

The school I attended from kindergarten through grade four was a one-room country school on the outskirts of Ann Arbor, Michigan. The small, white clapboard building, complete with large bell, hunkered with its flagpole and swing sets in the midst of small farms and apple orchards not far from the Huron River. One teacher taught all the grades, so that our fates were sealed with Miss Irwin's for as long as Miss Irwin lasted at Foster School #16 Fractional.

We began our day with the salute to the flag, under Gilbert Stuart's classic portrait of George Washington. From there we went on to lessons and lunch, then took naps with our heads down on our desks. We ended the day with square dancing. Miss Irwin was free to set the tone in any way she chose.

Much as I loved the dancing, I had trouble elsewhere early in my schooling. I had math anxiety, as it's come to be called. Letters, reading, spelling made sense to me, but numbers had such strange proclivities. That zero times four was zero, canceling the existence of the four, seemed dubious at best.

As I advanced through the higher grades, which took me, eventually, into the Ann Arbor public schools—there were four in my kindergarten and nine hundred in my graduating senior class—my math anxiety multiplied, so to speak. Even geometry, which my friends told me I'd be able to master, bollixed me. In college I avoided math and science whenever possible. I turned to arts and letters, where I felt on safer ground.

It troubled me throughout my education that I had to obey and perform for teachers whose judgment I didn't respect. I had a few teachers whom I respected enormously, a middling group of ordinary mortals, and finally an index of teachers I thought ill of, who nonetheless had the power to determine the course of my education and my life.

High school history, for example, was taught as an endless series of wars. When I got to the university and encountered social and intellectual history, the history that lives and breathes, I felt all the more resentful of my earlier training.

Our schooling makes us brave or timid, adept socially or not; it makes us team players or selfish players. Children may understand the larger implications of their classes long before they can articulate their feelings. So remember, when you urge your children to hurry lest they miss the bus, you urge them toward a complicated future, much of which is subject to random luck.

Snakes in This Grass?

WILMOT—"Dear Abutter," the letter begins. Anxiety grips any landowner at the sight of these words.

The letter describes our neighbor's plan to spread municipal sludge and industrial organic waste as he closes his gravel pit, mixing these substances with sand to produce topsoil capable of sustaining grass. He must, in accordance with state and federal laws, close the pit by grading, loaming, and seeding the area.

The ultimate picture is bucolic—rich hayfields surrounding Eagle Pond. But between the time the first ten-wheeler rumbles across the small bridge at the neck of the Blackwater River and the joyful mowing of good hay, we face uncertainty.

Not for nothing is our state's vehicular motto "Live Free or Die." The town of Wilmot, may it survive our depredations, has no ordinances regarding the stockpiling or spreading of municipal waste.

The municipal sludge is to come from Hanover and Concord. (Concord's smells worse than Hanover's: You may make of that what you will.)

The industrial wastes—the short paper fibers from a paper plant, and residue from the making of gelatine used in the photographic process—will be trucked in from Vermont and Massachusetts. One wonders why two out-of-state firms would trouble themselves to ship wastes such a distance. Could it be that the Granite State has looser regulations governing environmental matters?

While the town offers no impediment to the proposal, the state enforces regulations for the closure of sand and gravel pits. The area must be graded, loamed, and seeded to prevent erosion and to prevent an overabundance of nutrients from percolating into the water table. Dumping must be limited to an area 2,000 feet away from any body of water. Resource Conservation Services Inc. of Plymouth, our neighbor's consultant on technical matters, must obtain permission from the Water Supply and Pollution Control Division of the state's Department of Environmental Services before the project can proceed.

The DES rules sound reasonable. Resource Conservation Services of Plymouth assures us that the state guidelines will protect the area from ecological damage and that the sludge will not be toxic.

If we were not veterans of the pollution caused by the Turnkey Landfill operation in South Danbury, conducted on another portion of our neighbor's land, we might have more faith in a happy outcome for all parties. The landfill turned Jack Wells Brook, Eagle Pond, and the source of the Blackwater River into a copper-colored, stinking nightmare a few years back. What help were regulations to us then?

And here's something more that troubles me: Tests for toxicity will be conducted by the company managing the project.

Should ecological damage result from this enterprise, despite everybody's best intentions, who will clean up the mess? Will the mess *be* cleanable?

Suppose by some miracle the sludge contains no toxic waste (or an "acceptable amount," if such is possible). Suppose the stockpiling and spreading of the sludge proceeds according to regulations.

Then suppose that a large, noisy, dust-raising truck bearing its odoriferous load turns down Eagle Pond Road. Imagine that you live downwind of the proceedings, within a mile, as we do. Or imagine that you own Camps Kenwood and Evergreen on Eagle Pond, which four generations of children have enjoyed here in our sleepy portion of the globe. The camp shares a boundary with the land being reclaimed.

There is no way, *no way on earth,* that the stockpiling and spreading of sewage sludge and industrial waste will not compromise the very existence of the camp.

This is the time to protest. About twenty days remain before our neighbor secures permission to move ahead. Once we hear the sound of the first truck downshifting onto the pond road, any opposition will be too little and too late.

Reflections on a Roadside Warning

Be Prepared To Stop, says the orange sign at the bridge where Route 4 going west peels off from Route 11, near Andover. *One Lane Bridge Ahead,* says another.

For months now, all through the winter and spring and on into early summer, a crew has been taking up portions of the paving, reinforcing the structure, pouring concrete, and paving over the patch, gradually mending every support in the bridge. When I told a friend that we're having bridge work done, she assumed I meant trips to a dental emporium on Clinton Street. With people, as with bridges, after forty it's patch, patch, patch.

In winter, a plastic shelter protected the drillers and welders and hardening concrete from the worst cold. Trucks and trailers and two turquoise Porta-Johns have been stationed near the old Potter Place depot for months. Walkie-talkies in hand, familiar flagmen beckon us into the left lane to cross the bridge, or hold us while oncoming traffic swings into the right lane to cross. We begin to feel that we know the whole crew after all this time. Their pickups and trailers remind me of the gypsy caravans I've seen parked along rural English lanes.

Be Prepared To Stop. Sometimes as I wait my turn to cross, my mind waxes philosophical over these words. They describe this family's state of mind a year after my husband's second operation for cancer, six months after my mother's rib-cracking fall in the tub, a month after my mother-in-law's third ambulance trip to Yale New Haven Hospital within the year, and my own trip to New London Hospital with leg elevated, bath towel sopping up blood from a shrapnel-like wound after a freak accident with the lawn mower.

Be Prepared To Stop. Did we ever feel in charge of our lives? It was a delusion.

Folk wisdom says that trouble comes in threes, but I'd say it comes in multiples of three. We've become an anxiety-ridden family, and alas there's nothing remotely unusual about the condition. Our late, exceedingly dear minister, Jack Jensen, once gave a sermon on keeping cheerful. He said that he derived small comfort from thinking that others are worse off than we are: This idea simply adds guilt over our self-absorption to the suffering that provoked the original comparison. That seemed to me to have the ring of truth—to ring changes on truth.

Having to stop at the bridge is not inevitable, but it is likely between the hours of seven and three. On those occasions when I'm able to drive over unimpeded, my heart leaps up.

One day the reinforcement will be done, and we'll pass by without thinking of the delays and impatience of the last year. We'll see no more men dressed against all weathers, their breath rising in white plumes on bitter February mornings, or April rain dripping off the brims of their caps. No more will the welders hunch over their task, their faces protected from the heat and light of the welding by gear that makes them look like Japanese riot police. One of the men smokes a pipe, looking as if he'd wandered in from an English Department committee meeting. Recently I realized that I'm going to miss them.

Poetry and the Mail

Just as there are all kinds of teachers, CPAs, telephone operators, and particle physicists, there are all kinds of poets—tall and short, meticulous and sloppy, political and apolitical, sonneteers and writers of free verse. All poets share one thing, however—a daily dependence on the mail. "It is joy, and it is pain," as the great Russian poet Anna Akhmatova once said, though not about the mail.

Like the tides, white envelopes go out and come in again. Sometimes they bring bad news (on a printed rejection slip), sometimes good news ("We have decided to print all seven of your poems on dysfunctional relationships in a special issue.") and sometimes equivocal news ("Your book certainly deserves to be published, but as AT&T has raised its rates, we are not able to take on new authors at this time.") Almost everything important that happens to us happens through the mail.

Fellowships. Requests for permission to reprint a poem or set it to music. Money! Fan mail and its opposite. Reviews—gratifying, or annoying, or devastating. And of course the first copy of a new book, shining and fragrant, from the printer.

Once a letter was forwarded to me from the *New Republic*. It had come from the Sorbonne. How very kind, I thought—as I searched for the letter opener, so as not to mangle the return address—someone has taken the trouble to write me all the way from Paris. Well, it wasn't fan mail. The discerning professor mopped the floor with my poem. "Jejune" is the adjective forever present in my mind. Jejune comes from a Latin word that means fasting. Perhaps he had low blood sugar when he fashioned his note. Now every time I finish a poem I ask my-self, is this jejune?

Luckily such unpleasant moments are more than compensated for by kindness from complete strangers. Several times someone has writ-ten to tell me that one of my poems was read at the funeral of a rela-tive or friend, and that it was an immense comfort. Who could ask for more than that?

What a weird impulse writing is in the first place—to make some-thing out of memory and observation, out of emotion and thought, utterance and silence, the stated and the implied. *Out of nothing,* as a woman once said to me at a cocktail party. Yes, I thought to myself immodestly—just as God created the world. We try to say exactly what we mean, to put the exact word in the exact place—and then we take it out to the mailbox and put up the red flag.

After three or four weeks have passed, we begin to anticipate an answer. Pulses race as we approach the box. There it is! The self-addressed envelope, coming back with our fate printed on a form re-jection slip, or written on fancy stationery. We try to guess from the heft of the envelope whether all the poems have been returned, or if one or two have been accepted. We adopt the appearance of calm; we even open another letter or two before the critical envelope. Ah! They've taken *two* poems! But what was so bad about the *other* two?

If there are no ink marks or obscure stains on the returned poems, we slip them into another envelope, with an S.A.S.E., and send them out again—we all do it—and in a couple of weeks we begin the vigil, waiting for the sound of the mail-carrier's car.

IV

Notes on Literature and the Arts

Kicking the Eggs

My earliest recollections of Robert Bly date from my undergraduate days at the University of Michigan, in the late sixties. There were poetry readings every Tuesday in the undergraduate library—a great luxury, but of course we were not aware how great; we accepted them as our due. One day Robert strode into the room with Donald Hall, Robert wearing a serape, with a blue silk scarf around his neck. He began by reading a few poems from *Silence in the Snowy Fields,* including two permanent favorites of mine, "Hunting Pheasants in a Cornfield" and "Poem in Three Parts." Then he turned to work from *The Light Around the Body,* beginning with poems not overtly about the Vietnam War, but certainly about lives of Americans spent in wrong pursuits—"The Busy Man Speaks" and "Come with Me"; then he read some of the inward poems of the last section—"Looking into a Face," "When the Dumb Speak."

When he read "Counting Small-Boned Bodies," it was as if a sudden squall pulled up a huge tree, roots and all. We fell into his vision of apocalypse. At that reading I understood that W.H. Auden, when he wrote, "Poetry makes nothing happen," was wrong. Here was harrowing public indignation at our atrocities, our sightless, xenophobic, greedy, paranoid warmongering. I understood from that day, from Robert, that poetry is a public moral force, or can be, and not only a path into the individual human soul.

He came almost yearly to read at Michigan, staying with his old friend and confrere, Donald Hall—who by 1972 would be my spouse. I was among the young poets at Michigan who attended the parties after readings, and at these parties I observed the host and his guest tell stories, joke, squabble, show off, and discuss serious ideas earnestly.

Over the years they went through times of separation, even of estrangement, but they wrote endless letters, talked on the phone, helped each other with poems and prose. They couldn't divorce, no matter the schism: they seemed linked at the backbone. Robert went through his changes, Donald went through his—personal, political, aesthetic, philosophical—but they remain profoundly attached.

Once I took a photograph of them working together on each other's poems, sitting on our big yellow sofa in Ann Arbor. At least three people, glancing at that picture, have asked Donald, "Is that your mother?" (Robert turned gray before Don did.) Now what would Marie-Louise von Franz make of it?

In the years before Don and I were married, Don always made breakfast for his guest from Minnesota, or watched him, aghast, as he made his own. Once Robert dropped an egg while removing it from the carton. Donald cast a Puritan look, whereupon Robert kicked the raw egg gleefully under the refrigerator. "I'm a Capricorn!" he said.

It was Robert who urged me to translate Anna Akhmatova's poems, and who, along with Louis Simpson, appealed to Vera Dunham to work with me. Robert had come to visit us for a few days in New Hampshire. He asked what I was working on, read it thoughtfully. "It's time for you to choose a poet dead or alive and work with that poet as a master," he said. That way of reading had never occurred to me. "I cannot choose a man for a master," I said. "Then read Akhmatova," said Robert.

I gathered all the translations I could get my hands on, but felt that the poems remained hidden, obscured. I made my own versions for my own amusement, and as a way of close reading. Then I found a student of Comparative Literature at Dartmouth College, Lou Teel, who gave me literal versions of a few poems.

Next time Robert came to visit, he asked me what I was up to. I showed him my exercises, for that's what I considered them to be. He decided on the spot to do an Eighties Press book of them, and he urged me to work with Vera Dunham as co-translator.

For five years I sat at Akhmatova's feet. What Robert told me was true: Whatever work you put into translation comes back to you like the twelve baskets of bread and fish left after the feeding of the five thousand. It's to Robert that I owe the book, and to him the deep changes that occurred in my own poems as a result of that work.

There is no one else on earth like Robert Elwood Bly. He is a cross between William Blake, Ralph Nader, and Mr. Magoo, and I love and revere him endlessly.

A Proposal for New Hampshire Writers

These are lean times for writers. The NEA is under attack by conservative "politicos." Patrick Buchanan habitually refers to the NEA as the "upholstered playpen of the Eastern Liberal Establishment." I don't enjoy being compared to a baby in a playpen, however well-appointed. I'm an adult working artist, and I'm talking to my fellow adult working artists.

The school boards in our state are weighing the worth of arts programs, and, to most citizens, literature seems more expendable than physics, bookkeeping, computer skills, or even football. Literature, the garden of our inward life, loses its caretaker, and the water fails in the fountain when set against the demands of the outer life—the life of highway construction, stock reports, and medical technology.

In the days before the Primary, I made an informal canvas of the Democrats' views on funding for the NEA, censorship, and First Amendment rights. I got not a single authoritative answer. I was told by three staffers that someone with more expertise in the area would call me back. Not one called back. One young man in Clinton's office tried to bluster me, saying that Clinton is a strong supporter of the arts, but backing up the claim with a paucity of facts, some of them plain wrong. The telephone number information gave me for Jerry Brown turned out to be the number of a poor beleaguered resident of Bow, who has the misfortune to share the candidate's name. The point is that the arts aren't worth a callback.

My friends, my fellow artists, we must demonstrate to this society that if it is to be a civilization, and not just a raw heap of strivers after two cars and ski vacations, we must have art always before us. We must make our visions and gifts accessible to all. Everyone needs art, but not everyone knows it. Not everyone knows when they need to consume more calcium—they just know that they are sick, and can't figure out how they got that way. So with art. People must have it or they sicken. It is soul food.

Now, a proposition. Go to your local library and offer to do a reading of your own work, or the work of others. Gratis. This time, gratis. Gather two or three writers and make the same offer. Experiment with choral reading; include the audience. Offer an evening for children. Make sure the reader has a rocking chair, a big old lamp, a rag rug, and that the children have big pillows on which to lounge—on which to "loaf, and invite their souls." Encourage parents to bring the kids in their pajamas.

If you don't feel comfortable putting yourself forward, read the work of Emily Dickinson, Anton Chekhov, Margaret Wise Brown, E. B. White. Adults love *Charlotte's Web* every bit as much as children do. Read a play with three or four other performers. Get someone to play haunting melodies between acts . . . Wear something wacky: wear a mask, get down on the floor with kids and tell them myths. Stand on your head and recite "Uncle William"—just DO IT.

Art is for everybody. It doesn't disappear when money disappears. It's a permanent treasure, not something that is not even worth a phone call. We're the ones to remind people of that. We are the keepers of the flame, if you will. Our job is to see that the flame not only doesn't go out, but that it shines in the windows of the library or town hall or grange for one or two or three evenings in the coming months.

Thoughts on the Gifts of Art

How do we justify the need for art in these troubled economic times, when budgets are being slashed, jobs lost, the physical health and safety of our citizens compromised? What's our excuse for existing, and for needing money from the government to continue our work?

I think of it this way: that the media—the papers, magazines, TV, radio—bring us news of the outer life. What's the government up to, where will the next mall spring up or the next solid waste disposal site, where's the latest outbreak of war and acute misery, what's the latest discovery in physics or medicine?

Artists report on the inner life, and the inner life distinguishes us from centipedes, although I may underestimate centipedes. The love of the absolute beauty of art, the longing for the well-being of the planet and all its creatures, the awe we feel in the face of life and death, the delights of the inward eye and inward ear, the understanding and nurture of the soul—these are the gifts of art. In a way every piece of art, every performance, is a state-of-the-soul address.

We cannot afford to ignore our inner lives, our imaginations, for when we do, we become capable of extreme cruelty and destruction. "Tenderness toward existence," in the poet Galway Kinnell's lovely phrase, is what we lose when we lose art, or when we fail to value it properly.

Recent work by Yale psychiatrist Jerome Singer suggests that people whose imaginative lives are active commit fewer violent crimes, are more creative, and are more tolerant of human diversity. Art fosters the life of the imagination. How can this society afford not to foster art?

Everything I Know About Writing Poetry

(Notes for a Lecture)*

1. Why do we want to write poems? What is behind this crazy impulse? The wish to connect with others, on a deep level, about inward things.

The pressure of emotion, which many people prefer to ignore, but which, for you, is the very substance of your work, your *clay*.

There's play involved in the writing of poetry. Baby waking up. We have to be like babies waking up—trying every sound, every pitch, every word, however nonsensical. Later, be a revising adult. Babies build it up and knock it down again.

There's the need to make sense of life behind the impulse to write.

And finally, we celebrate the world by writing about it, we observe it more closely, with more love. We are more fully alive and aware because of our efforts.

2. So where do we begin. We feel this pressure of emotion and thought, and we need to find, among the many things of this world, a way to *body forth* our feeling. It's metaphor, the engine of poetry, that does the work for us. Metaphor is simply talking about one thing in terms of another. Take any Robert Frost poem.

"Two roads diverged in a yellow wood,/ And sorry I could not travel both/ And be one traveler, long I stood/ And looked down one as far as I could/ To where it bent in the undergrowth . . ." Two

---

*Delivered in 1991 at a literary conference in Enfield, New Hampshire.

divergences, an inner and an outer. The thing—the image—does the work of carrying feeling. Ezra Pound once said, "The natural object is always the adequate symbol." Believe it, act on it, and your poems will not fly off into abstraction. A few more examples of the working image, what Eliot called the "objective correlative"—that is, an outward sign of an inward state.

> The hare limp'd trembling through the frozen grass.
> *Keats "Eve of St. Agnes"*

> I put my left glove on my right hand . . .
> *A. A. "Song of the Last Meeting"*

> By the gate now, the moss is grown, the different mosses
> Too deep to clear them away!
> *Pound's tr. "The River Merchant's Wife"*

I want to read a couple of perfectly realized poems—perfectly imagined—poems in which the inner world is revealed in terms of the outer world—revealed in terms of things. The natural object is always . . .

[Here Jane read aloud Elizabeth Bishop's "Crusoe in England" and Ezra Pound's translation "The River Merchant's Wife: A Letter"]

3. Find fresh language. Snow blanketed the field. Not good enough. Pound said, "Make it new." Make it specific rather than general. Don't say there were a few things on the desk when you can say there were three letters on the desk, one opened in haste without a letter opener . . . You cannot do without a thesaurus. The word comes from the Latin meaning *treasure*. Also an OED.

3a. Omit useless words.

4. Tell the whole truth. Don't be lazy, don't be afraid. Close the critic out when you are drafting something new. Take chances in the interest of clarity of emotion.

5. The "so what" test.

6. Revise.

7. Develop a tough snout. Even established writers get rejected all the time.

8. Be a good steward of your gifts. Protect your time. Feed your inner life. Avoid too much noise. Read good books, have good sentences in your ears. Be by yourself as often as you can. Walk. Take the phone off the hook. Work regular hours.

V

Interviews

❧

An Interview with Bill Moyers *(1993)*

MOYERS: Your poems on moving—on leaving one place and arriving in another—rang true with me because they express a sense of being lost I have experienced even when I know where I am. How did you come to write these?

KENYON: I think that writing those was my effort to understand and control what was happening to me. For me poetry's a safe place always, a refuge, and it has been since I took it up in the eighth grade, so it was natural for me to write about these things that were going on in my own soul.

MOYERS: What *was* going on?

KENYON: I felt quite disembodied for a while. Someone said that when you move, it takes your soul a few weeks to catch up with you. Of course, this house is so thoroughly full of Don's family, his ancestors, their belongings, their reverberations, that when we came here, I felt almost annihilated by the "otherness" of it at times.

MOYERS: When I read "Here" I'm struck by the paradox that it was you who persuaded Don to come back to New Hampshire, it was you who imagined a future here.

Here

You always belonged here.
You were theirs, certain as a rock.
I'm the one who worries

145

if I fit in with the furniture
and the landscape.
                            But I "follow too much
the devices and desires of my own heart."

Already the curves in the road
are familiar to me, and the mountain
in all kinds of light,
treating all people the same.
And when I come over the hill,
I see the house, with its generous
and firm proportions, smoke
rising gaily from the chimney.

I feel my life start up again,
like a cutting when it grows
the first pale and tentative
root hair in a glass of water.

KENYON: I did, strange to say. I guess I didn't know what I was saying
when I said it. I was born in Ann Arbor, but my family lived outside
the city limits and I went to a one-room school until I was in the fifth
grade when the township was annexed into the Ann Arbor city
schools, so I grew up in the country. The farm across the road was a
working farm, and all the smells and sounds of country existence were
familiar and dear to me. When I grew older, there was a gradual ero-
sion of that existence as the road was paved and the town of Ann
Arbor crept out to where my family was living. So coming here was
like recovering something for me that was very, very dear.

MOYERS: And yet in the beginning you felt like a stranger.

KENYON: I did, but I think that's natural.

MOYERS: In "From Room to Room," how does the mind go from singing "the tie that binds" down the road at the church to the astronauts in the heavens?

From Room to Room

Here in this house, among photographs
of your ancestors, their hymnbooks and old
shoes . . .
        I move from room to room,
a little dazed, like the fly. I watch it
bump against each window.

I am clumsy here, thrusting
slabs of maple into the stove.
Out of my body for a while,
weightless in space . . .
        Sometimes
the wind against the clapboard
sounds like a car driving up to the house.

My people are not here, my mother
and father, my brother. I talk
to the cats about weather.

"Blessed be the tie that binds . . ."
we sing in the church down the road.
And how does it go from there? The tie . . .

the tether, the hose carrying
oxygen to the astronaut,
turning, turning outside the hatch,
taking a look around.

KENYON: It's really a visual image of the astronaut floating out with his umbilical cord from the mother ship.

MOYERS: Women are always doing this, aren't they? They move from their place to their husband's place, from their ground to his ground. When I read these poems I think of my own wife, Judith, who moved with me from pillar to post, from Texas to Scotland to Washington to New York. I imagined her when I read "Finding a Long Gray Hair."

Finding a Long Gray Hair

I scrub the long floorboards
in the kitchen, repeating
the motions of other women
who have lived in this house.
And when I find a long gray hair
floating in the pail,
I feel my life added to theirs.

KENYON: It's funny how working in a place and perhaps changing it a little is a way of making it yours. I've patched and sanded and painted and scraped and raked and shoveled. That was the way I gradually came to feel that this was my place too. I think making my gardens—I have enormous perennial gardens—was probably the thing that finally really tied me to this place.

MOYERS: Why is the natural world so important to you?

KENYON: I love it so much. I always have. I think growing up in the country far from friends made me an inward child to begin with. I can remember playing long hours outside by myself.

MOYERS: Did you really know at the age of eight that you wanted to be a poet?

KENYON: Heavens, no!

MOYERS: When did that insight come to you?

KENYON: That's something that I almost feel spooky about saying. Even now calling myself a poet seems, somehow, to step out of line.

MOYERS: Why?

KENYON: I guess it's not for me to say somehow.

MOYERS: But you write poems.

KENYON: I guess I do.

MOYERS: You just got a Guggenheim fellowship for your poems, and I've seen people respond to your poems at the poetry festival. But something holds you back from claiming what you've done.

KENYON: There *is,* and I don't know quite what it is. I mean, at a party if someone asks, "What do you do?" I think, "Oh, dear," and say, "Well, I'm a writer." Then they say, "What do you write?" and I say, "I'm a poet." A funny look comes across their face at that point and they say, "Have you published?" When I say, "Yes, I have published," they tell me about *their* beginning efforts at poetry and how they no longer have time to read poetry, and we go from there.

MOYERS: What does it say that many of us want to be poets and yet, as a society, we scarcely honor poets, even dead poets?

KENYON: I think people imagine that poets live a kind of exalted existence, which we don't. We have the same problems that everybody else has. I don't know why people like to imagine that they could write poems. I think it's partly because everyone uses language.

MOYERS: We all have something to say.

KENYON: Yes. We all have something to say, and we all use language, so people think that they themselves could do this. It's like the mother who says, looking at Picasso's paintings, "My child draws better than that." People don't know how hard it is to write, what a struggle it is to know what you want to say and then to say what you mean.

MOYERS: How long does it take you to write a poem?

KENYON: Usually for me it's a process of at least three or four months. I work with several other writers. Of course, Don and I exchange work and help each other a good deal. But there are two other writers with whom I work very closely, and we meet two or three, sometimes four, times a year and go over everything we've written together.

We sit down and read and talk about every single line and then I go home and finish something. So if I've started something relatively close to workshop, I may be able to finish the poem within a month or two. But if there's a long break between workshops, then I'm kind of held up until I take it through workshop. I would never consider sending anything out until my friends have looked at it.

MOYERS: They're your first editors?

KENYON: Yes. I really have three first readers. Don's my first reader always. I listen to everything he says, as I listen to everything my friends tell me, and then finally I have to decide for myself what really needs to be changed and what really can't be changed.

MOYERS: You both gave up a lot when you moved to New Hampshire. Don gave up tenure, insurance, retirement, pension plan, all the amenities that come with an established university position. Does choosing the life of the poet require a vow of poverty?

KENYON: It requires a life of as much simplicity as possible, but far from being impoverished by coming here, we have both been incalculably enriched in our inner lives by becoming part of this community.

MOYERS: When did you know that you were at home here?

KENYON: I'd say I began to feel at home here within eight or ten months.

MOYERS: Did writing poetry help you to settle in?

KENYON: I'm sure it did. You see, when we moved here, I had absolutely unstructured time. I had twenty-four hours a day to do or not do what I wanted. So I really began to work seriously as a poet when we came here.

MOYERS: Long hours every day?

KENYON: Not long hours. Two or three hours of intensive work on poems are about as much as I can do. Writing poems is spilling your guts, and you can't sustain that over hours.

MOYERS: In talking to poets about their work I've noticed there comes a moment when their emotional exhaustion is evident.

KENYON: Yes. Poetry has an intensity about it, which is one of its loveliest qualities, but that's also the thing that fatigues you when you're working on it. There's a pitch of emotion in poems that you must rise to. Every time you work on the poem you must rise to it again.

MOYERS: It's such a way of remembering, and remembering what it is you want to hold on to is very difficult to do at times. I am reminded of "February: Thinking of Flowers." Is that poem a deliberate effort to break through the melancholy of winter?

February: Thinking of Flowers

Now wind torments the field,
turning the white surface back

on itself, back and back on itself,
like an animal licking a wound.

Nothing but white—the air, the light;
only one brown milkweed pod
bobbing in the gully, smallest
brown boat on the immense tide.

A single green sprouting thing
would restore me. . . .

Then think of the tall delphinium,
swaying, or the bee when it comes
to the tongue of the burgundy lily.

KENYON: Dreaming of gardens is something that always elevates my
mood.

MOYERS: What do you mean by "greedy for unhappiness" in "De-
pression in Winter"?

Depression in Winter

There comes a little space between the south
side of a boulder
and the snow that fills the woods around it.
Sun heats the stone, reveals
a crescent of bare ground: brown ferns,
and tufts of needles like red hair,
acorns, a patch of moss, bright green. . . .

I sank with every step up to my knees,
throwing myself forward with a violence

of effort, greedy for unhappiness—
until by accident I found the stone,
with its secret porch of heat and light,
where something small could luxuriate, then
turned back down my path, chastened and calm.

KENYON: Do you ever get into a state where you just need to let it go?
I find that when I feel that way I do something. I desert myself physi-
cally in some way and that lets the steam off without hurting anybody
I care about.

MOYERS: I know people who welcome melancholy.

KENYON: Yes. Then they know where they are. There are moments, I
think, when we all feel that. Depression is something I've suffered
from all my life. I'm manic-depressive, actually, and I was not prop-
erly diagnosed until I was thirty-eight years old. In my case it's more
like a unipolar depression. Manic-depression usually involves both
poles of feeling. That is, when you're happy you're too happy, when
you're sad you get too sad. Mine behaves almost like a serious depres-
sion only and I rarely become manic.

MOYERS: Depression is really the land of the living dead.

KENYON: It surely is.

MOYERS: It must be hard to read poems about depression in public.

KENYON: It can be.

MOYERS: How do audiences respond?

KENYON: I find people are usually moved by them, and many people,
even if they've never experienced such unhappiness themselves, know
people who have. Either they have parents or siblings or spouses or
friends who have been touched by mood disorders. I have found that

when I've read any of these poems that really dwell on depression, people come up to me afterward and hug me. They say, for example, "My mother was manic-depressive, and I had a terrible childhood because of it." As I was reading "Having It Out with Melancholy" last week in Louisville, Kentucky, a man in the second row, who had been looking at me intently as the poem went on and it talks about unrelenting depression, took his hand and put it over his heart. Then he brought his hand to his heart over and over and just looked in my face. I knew that he also suffered.

Having It Out with Melancholy *

*If many remedies are prescribed for an illness,
you may be certain that the illness has no cure.*
A. P. CHEKHOV
The Cherry Orchard

1 FROM THE NURSERY

When I was born, you waited
behind a pile of linen in the nursery,
and when we were alone, you lay down
on top of me, pressing
the bile of desolation into every pore.

And from that day on
everything under the sun and moon
made me sad—even the yellow
wooden beads that slid and spun
along a spindle on my crib.

---

* *The Language of Life,* like the original television program, used only a part of the poem; this is the whole poem.

You taught me to exist without gratitude.
You ruined my manners toward God:
"We're here simply to wait for death;
the pleasures of earth are overrated."

I only appeared to belong to my mother,
to live among blocks and cotton undershirts
with snaps; among red tin lunch boxes
and report cards in ugly brown slipcases.
I was already yours—the anti-urge,
the mutilator of souls.

2   BOTTLES

Elavil, Ludiomil, Doxepin,
Norpramin, Prozac, Lithium, Xanax,
Wellbutrin, Parnate, Nardil, Zoloft.
The coated ones smell sweet or have
no smell; the powdery ones smell
like the chemistry lab at school
that made me hold my breath.

3   SUGGESTION FROM A FRIEND

You wouldn't be so depressed
if you really believed in God.

4   OFTEN

Often I go to bed as soon after dinner
as seems adult
(I mean I try to wait for dark)

in order to push away
from the massive pain in sleep's
frail wicker coracle.

5   ONCE THERE WAS LIGHT

Once, in my early thirties, I saw
that I was a speck of light in the great
river of light that undulates through time.

I was floating with the whole
human family. We were all colors—those
who are living now, those who have died,
those who are not yet born. For a few

moments I floated, completely calm,
and I no longer hated having to exist.

Like a crow who smells hot blood
you came flying to pull me out
of the glowing stream.
"I'll hold you up. I never let my dear
ones drown!" After that, I wept for days.

6   IN AND OUT

The dog searches until he finds me
upstairs, lies down with a clatter
of elbows, puts his head on my foot.

Sometimes the sound of his breathing
saves my life—in and out, in
and out; a pause, a long sigh. . . .

7 PARDON

A piece of burned meat
wears my clothes, speaks
in my voice, dispatches obligations
haltingly, or not at all.
It is tired of trying
to be stouthearted, tired
beyond measure.

We move on to the monoamine
oxidase inhibitors. Day and night
I feel as if I had drunk six cups
of coffee, but the pain stops
abruptly. With the wonder
and bitterness of someone pardoned
for a crime she did not commit
I come back to marriage and friends,
to pink-fringed hollyhocks; come back
to my desk, books, and chair.

8 CREDO

Pharmaceutical wonders are at work
but I believe only in this moment
of well-being. Unholy ghost,
you are certain to come again.

Coarse, mean, you'll put your feet
on the coffee table, lean back,
and turn me into someone who can't
take the trouble to speak; someone
who can't sleep, or who does nothing

but sleep; can't read, or call
for an appointment for help.

There is nothing I can do
against your coming.
When I awake, I am still with thee.

9   WOOD THRUSH

High on Nardil and June light
I wake at four,
waiting greedily for the first
notes of the wood thrush. Easeful air
presses through the screen
with the wild, complex song
of the bird, and I am overcome

by ordinary contentment.
What hurt me so terribly
all my life until this moment?
How I love the small, swiftly
beating heart of the bird
singing in the great maples;
its bright, unequivocal eye.

MOYERS: I believe your poems help people to deal with depression.

KENYON: That is my hope, because if this is just personal, then I've
been wasting my time. The unrelenting quality of depression really
makes its impression on people. It's this thing that will not let you go,
that comes when it wants and goes when it wants. You're like a chip-
munk in the eagle's talons. There's nothing you can do. Well, that's

not strictly true. There is something you can do if you have mood disorders. There are medications that help people.

MOYERS: And are you on medication?

KENYON: Oh, yes. I'm on a lot of medication. I'm on a combination of medications, and I jokingly call my psychiatrist my "mixologist." He's a good man.

MOYERS: When you write "I was already yours," you mean depression? Depression owned you?

KENYON: Yes. There is a genetic component to this. My father had it, and I believe his mother had it. I really take after my father's people. I'm sure that it came down his lines. I'm trying to explain to people who have never experienced this kind of desolation, what it is. It's important for people to understand that those with endogenous depression, melancholia, don't do this for the fun of it. I'm no more responsible for my melancholy than I am for having brown eyes. Unfortunately, it's taken me a long time to really believe that it's not my fault. It's like having heart disease or diabetes. I've decided that I want to increase people's understanding about this disease. I want to ease people's burdens.

MOYERS: Well, you do just that when you say, "I go to bed as soon after dinner / as seems adult / (I mean I try to wait for dark)." My own brother suffered from depression. I have had occasional bouts with it. How many times have we wanted to go to bed without being able to explain to anybody? When I read that, I thought, "She's got it."

KENYON: There are lots of people in public life who have had serious mood disorders. Abraham Lincoln was depressive.

MOYERS: Lyndon Johnson suffered bouts of melancholy.

KENYON: See, anybody who's anybody is manic-depressive.

MOYERS: I'll let the audience decide, but I appreciate the courage it takes for you to address it.

KENYON: Well, it's either courage or I don't know what.

MOYERS: Tell me about "Once There Was Light."

KENYON: I really had a vision of that once. It was like a waking dream. My eyes were open and I saw these rooms, this house, but in my mind's eye, or whatever language you can find to say these things, I also saw a great ribbon of light and every human life was suspended. There was no struggle. There was only this buoyant shimmering, undulating stream of light. I took my place in this stream and after that my life changed fundamentally. I relaxed into existence in a way that I never had before.

MOYERS: Relaxed into existence?

KENYON: Having had lifelong struggles with depression, there have been long periods in my life when being in this world hasn't seemed like any great bargain, but after having this wave of buoyant emotion, my understanding was changed fundamentally.

MOYERS: What happens at the end of that poem?

KENYON: It's a kind of personification of the return of this awful feeling, in the midst of this joy that I was momentarily experiencing. I realize, in retrospect, that this was probably a manic swing followed by a crash, a bad one.

MOYERS: When you crashed, would drugs bring you back?

KENYON: Yes, very gradually. They take a long time to work, and there are sometimes false starts with drugs. Sometimes you begin on a course of treatment with a drug that ultimately you're just not going to be able to tolerate. They all have some nasty side effects, and it's always a question of balancing side effects against the good that comes of them. Sometimes a drug just doesn't work for you. There's no way of knowing except by trying. It can take months to get straightened around. I went off all drugs this summer for the first time in eleven years, because I thought to myself, "I need to find out if I really need this stuff, or if I'm just pouring money down the drain." I went off everything. I tapered off and by June I was off everything. Five weeks later I crashed and it took us seven months to find the right drug in the right dose. I didn't write for seven months. I couldn't concentrate. I couldn't read. I didn't answer my mail. I didn't want to see friends.

MOYERS: Was it only medication that brought you back? Is it only medication that keeps you going?

KENYON: We don't know. In the years before I used antidepressants, I would sometimes have a kind of spontaneous relief from depressions. Who knows what happens in the brain? But I really seem to need these drugs.

MOYERS: What else has helped you?

KENYON: My belief in God, such as it is, especially the idea that a believer is part of the body of Christ, has kept me from harming myself. When I really didn't want to be conscious, didn't want to be aware, was in so much pain that I didn't want to be awake or aware, I've thought to myself, "If you injure yourself you're injuring the body of Christ, and Christ has been injured enough."

MOYERS: What about the little church here in town? You and Don are regulars there.

KENYON: Oh, that's a long and complex relationship. We began going to church when we moved here, and I had not been to church since I was twelve years old. I was brought up in the Methodist church in Ann Arbor, a large, rather rich suburban church, but my parents very much enjoyed the minister and so we went. Both of them had grown up in Methodist families. In fact, we have Methodist preachers on both sides.

MOYERS: Now there could be the cause of your depression!

KENYON: That could be! I have schoolmarms and Methodist ministers. But at the age of twelve I announced that I was too sophisticated for that kind of thing, whereupon the entire family stopped going to church. So I had not been in a church except for weddings, funerals, and baptisms since that time.

Then when we came here Don said, "Well, they'll be expecting us at church," and I thought, "Oh, this means putting on stockings and not lazing about reading the paper all day." Well, off we went. There was a wonderful minister who became a dear friend. That day he gave a shapely, intelligent, convincing sermon and I thought to myself, "I wouldn't mind going back and hearing him again." We got into the habit of going to church, and at first it was more a social act that a spiritual act. But within a short time I discovered that I had an enormous spiritual hunger that I knew nothing about. It had been stirred a little by Robert Bly in the late '60s and early '70s. I could sense in Bly the power of the sublime. He was in touch with some power that was thrilling. I began to see that the spiritual dimension that poetry could have, an almost priestly function for the poet, was the only spirituality I had known for a long time. Then we started going to church and, before I knew what had happened to me, I'd become a believer, which I really never was as a child. I dutifully said my prayers when I was a child, but I was afraid of that God. The God that our minister here talked about in his sermons was a God who overcomes you with love, not a God of rules and prohibitions. This was a God who, if you ask, forgives you no matter how far down in the well you are. If I didn't believe that I couldn't live.

MOYERS: Can you write a poem or think about faith when you're depressed?

KENYON: I do think about faith and I have been able to revise when I'm depressed, but I don't initiate things when I'm depressed. I can't call the plumber to come and fix the drain. I can't initiate anything. I can't move.

MOYERS: But you can think about your faith?

KENYON: Well, I can call out.

MOYERS: And do you get an answer?

KENYON: Sometimes I do. When you get to be my age and you've lived with depression for a number of years, you begin to have a context for believing that you will feel better at some point. You have been through it enough times so that you know, sooner or later, if you can just stick it out, it's going to lift. It's going to be better.

MOYERS: That might explain "Peonies at Dusk."

Peonies at Dusk

White peonies blooming along the porch
send out light
while the rest of the yard grows dim.

Outrageous flowers as big as human
heads! They're staggered
by their own luxuriance: I had
to prop them up with stakes and twine.

The moist air intensifies their scent,
and the moon moves around the barn
to find out what it's coming from.

In the darkening June evening
I draw a blossom near, and bending close
search it as a woman searches
a loved one's face.

KENYON: Gardening is something that has helped me. Gardening and hiking, exercise, being outside, that's all very important.

MOYERS: I know what you mean. When the claustrophobia of the city sets in and the darkness of winter is all around us, my wife and I begin to think of spring and her own flowers and plants. That's why I think this poem is one of my favorites. I really like that notion of concentrating on the blossom. It reminds me of meditation, paying attention.

KENYON: Yes. Being awake. I suppose that the men in the white coats would come and get me if they could hear me in my garden talking to my plants and saying, "What is it you need, my dear? Your leaves are turning yellow. Is the soil too alkaline for you? Do you need nitrogen? What's the problem?" When the roses are blooming and the peonies are blooming, I literally just say, "My beauties." I talk to them. I really do. It's nuts, but . . .

MOYERS: We should all be so nutty. So many people now live lives remote from "Peonies at Dusk."

KENYON: One of the functions of poetry is to keep the memory of people and places and things and happenings alive.

MOYERS: There's a curious passage perhaps related to this question in "The Bat." You're writing about this creature people habitually shun when suddenly the third person of the Trinity, the Holy Spirit, enters the poem.

The Bat

I was reading about rationalism,
the kind of thing we do up north
in early winter, where the sun
leaves work for the day at 4:15.

Maybe the world *is* intelligible
to the rational mind;
and maybe we light the lamps at dusk
for nothing. . . .

Then I heard wings overhead.

The cats and I chased the bat
in circles—living room, kitchen,
pantry, kitchen, living room. . . .
At every turn it evaded us

like the identity of the third person
in the Trinity: the one
who spoke through the prophets,
the one who astounded Mary
by suddenly coming near.

KENYON: What I had in mind was being broken in upon, the way
Mary was broken in upon by Gabriel. You think you're alone and sud-
denly there's this thing coming near you, so near that you can feel the
wind from the brushing of its wings. Why this experience with the
bat made me think of Mary and Gabriel, I don't know, but it did.

MOYERS: That's the point, isn't it? Inspiration occurs without expla-
nation.

KENYON: There are times when I just feel I'm being *given* poems.

MOYERS: How do we cultivate that in ourselves?

KENYON: We have to get quiet. We have to be still, and that's harder and harder in this century.

MOYERS: Has it ever occurred to you, and I don't mean this as perversely as it sounds, that perhaps depression is itself a gift, a kind of garden in which ideas grow and in which experiences take root?

KENYON: That may be because—I never thought of it this way—depression makes me still.

MOYERS: All through history it's been the people in retreat, those who go into stillness, who hear that voice.

KENYON: Yes. I use a long portion of the 139th Psalm as a sort of epigraph to *Constance*. The psalmist says, darkness and light, it's all the same. It's all from God. It's all in God, through God, with God. There is no place I can go where Your love does not pursue me. The poems in this book are very dark, and many of them I can't read without weeping. I can't read many of them when I do poetry readings, but there is something in me that will not be snuffed out, even by this awful disease.

MOYERS: How did you receive the word of Don's cancer?

KENYON: Well, at first with disbelief. You know, Kübler-Ross's five steps. At first there was disbelief, then there was a lot of howling around here.

MOYERS: Howling?

KENYON: Yes. Not a Yankee trait, but there was a lot of howling around here. And, well, what we have is the present. That's all we ever had, really, except for memory. So we're trying to learn to live in the present.

MOYERS: You wrote "Pharaoh" after Don's experience. Why did you call him "Pharaoh?"

Pharaoh

"The future ain't what it used to be,"
said the sage of the New York Yankees
as he pounded his mitt, releasing
the red dust of the infield
into the harshly illuminated evening air.

Big hands. Men with big hands
make things happen. The surgeon,
when I asked how big your tumor was,
held forth his substantial fist
with its globed class ring.

Home again, we live as charily as strangers.
Things are off: Touch rankles, food
is not good. Even the kindness of friends
turns burdensome; their flowers sadden
us, so many and so fair.

I woke in the night to see your
diminished bulk lying beside me—
you on your back, like a sarcophagus
as your feet held up the covers. . . .
The things you might need in the next
life surrounded you—your comb and glasses,
water, a book and a pen.

KENYON: This was an actual visual perception. He was lying in bed with the covers over him and his feet were holding up the covers at the bottom. I could see the outline of his body dimly in the dark room. This was after he was home and recovering from his big surgery, and it suggested to me a pharaoh, a sarcophagus.

MOYERS: A sarcophagus? A tomb?

KENYON: Yes. It's odd but true that there really is consolation from sad poems, and it's hard to know how that happens. There's the pleasure of the thing itself, the pleasure of the poem, and somehow it works against the sadness.

MOYERS: We now know that grief can be a consolation if you work through it therapeutically, and a poem can help us do that, though not by sugar-coated optimism or denial.

KENYON: No. Certainly not by denial.

MOYERS: I admire your attitude toward denial and the notion of living in the present which comes with it. You catch both so beautifully in "Otherwise." Is this a late poem, written after Don's illness? But didn't you have cancer also?

Otherwise

I got out of bed
on two strong legs.
It might have been
otherwise. I ate
cereal, sweet
milk, ripe, flawless
peach. It might
have been otherwise.

I took the dog uphill
to the birch wood.
All morning I did
the work I love.

At noon I lay down
with my mate. It might
have been otherwise.
We ate dinner together
at a table with silver
candlesticks. It might
have been otherwise.
I slept in a bed
in a room with paintings
on the walls, and
planned another day
just like this day.
But one day, I know,
it will be otherwise.

KENYON: Yes. I had a cancerous salivary gland removed from my neck about seven years ago, and I believe I wrote "Otherwise" before we knew about his metastasis, before we knew about his liver cancer. After the first bout but before the second.

MOYERS: Well, the first was bad enough, wasn't it?

KENYON: Yes, the first was plenty bad. He's had two big surgeries, but he has enormous human vitality and sprang back very well.

MOYERS: Do you and Don talk about death?

KENYON: Yes, we've talked very openly about our fears and our angers and our sorrows.

MOYERS: Do you see new subjects, new horizons for your work?

KENYON: I have been going through a time of poor concentration. I think it's partly to do with the upheaval in our lives from Don's illness and his mother's illness, and then my mother had a bad fall in October. So there've been a lot of upheavals in my personal life that have broken my concentration. I'm not in a good rhythm of work. But I think that also happens to me when I'm getting ready to make some kind of leap, either in the subjects I undertake to talk about in my poems or some technical change, maybe longer lines or something else—I don't know. These silences often come over me before something new breaks in, but they're hard to wait out.

MOYERS: How did you come to write "Let Evening Come"? So many people say that's their favorite of your poems.

Let Evening Come

Let the light of late afternoon
shine through chinks in the barn, moving
up the bales as the sun moves down.

Let the cricket take up chafing
as a woman takes up her needles
and her yarn. Let evening come.

Let dew collect on the hoe abandoned
in long grass. Let the stars appear
and the moon disclose her silver horn.

Let the fox go back to its sandy den.
Let the wind die down. Let the shed
go black inside. Let evening come.

To the bottle in the ditch, to the scoop
in the oats, to air in the lung
let evening come.

Let it come, as it will, and don't
be afraid. God does not leave us
comfortless, so let evening come.

KENYON: That poem was given to me.

MOYERS: By?

KENYON: The muse, the Holy Ghost. I had written all the other
poems in the book in which it appears, and I knew that it was a very
sober book. I felt it needed something redeeming. I went upstairs one
day with the purpose of writing something redeeming, which is not
the way to write, but this just fell out. I really didn't have to struggle
with it.

MOYERS: Do you still believe what that poem expresses, given Don's
cancer and your own illness?

KENYON: Yes. There are things in this life that we must endure which
are all but unendurable, and yet I feel that there is a great goodness.
Why, when there could have been nothing, is there something? This
is a great mystery. How, when there could have been nothing, does it
happen that there is love, kindness, beauty?

An Interview with David Bradt (March 1993)

BRADT: How did the Guggenheim fellowship you won last year affect your life?

KENYON: I was immensely heartened by it. I can't tell you what a thrill it was for me to look at the directory of Guggenheim fellows. To be listed with astrophysicists and dancers and mathematicians and novelists—every kind of human endeavor—was the biggest thrill. Winning has been such a support to me, more than financial, by far. What it says to me is that it matters whether I bother to work or not, whether I bother to build that fire in the stove and warm up the room and get going. It matters.

It came at a time just before Don knew that he was sick. We had three days of unalloyed happiness before we found that he was going to have to have more than half his liver out. While he was mending, I lived in the Upper Valley Hostel, a cooperative house where people stay who are in treatment or whose family members are in treatment. I spent all my time at the hospital, except when I was sleeping. The Guggenheim sustained me through all that. Then, starting in June, and running for seven months, I couldn't write. I don't know what happened. I was tired from all the stress. It wasn't just Don's illness. His mother had a heart attack. We went to Connecticut while Don was still recupuerating, and when she came home from the hospital, I took care of her. So I was taking care of Don and taking care of his mother. Then in early autumn, my mother had a bad fall, and I took care of her here for twelve days. All the time I was doing these other things, the thought that I had a Guggenheim kept me going. It said to me, "Okay, you're going to work again, and we hope you will go back to work when you can." It sustained me through terrible times.

BRADT: In your "Proposal for New Hampshire Writers" you talk about these as lean times for writers in terms of the political climate. How do you see politics affecting the arts in general?

KENYON: A governor or president who actively encourages the arts makes a difference—in the schools and in public gatherings such as the inaugural. A public official who thinks to include the arts is important to us as working artists. I think we have a good advocate in the White House now. Things are definitely looking up. We're hoping that Clinton's appointment to chair the National Endowment for the Arts will be a good person.

The Bush administration was not friendly to the arts. Bush's appointed chair at the Endowment was a disaster. By the end of her term she was vetoing anything with sexual content. Moderate Republicans were bullied by the conservative right—the born-agains and Southern conservative legislators. There were a number of encounters between the Endowment and the conservative right. The Mapplethorpe incident was just one. People don't want to fund something that makes them uncomfortable. I guess I can understand that, but I don't agree with it. Art does challenge us, and sometimes makes us uncomfortable.

BRADT: It should, shouldn't it?

KENYON: Yes, it should. Obviously as an artist I want to see art funded, but I can see the other point of view. There are people who really don't want to confront the things that serious artists confront. I think of certain people in this town, taxpaying citizens, and I wonder, could I in good conscience ask Dot to pay for art that is on the edge? But art is the mirror of the soul, individual and national. It tells us who we are, where we're going, what's valuable and what isn't.

BRADT: In light of recent political history, do you think writers and artists have an obligation to take political stands?

KENYON: Yes. Politics, when it gets into art, may not make for the best art, but any thinking person in this nation has to be political. If you're going to complain, then you better vote. If you're going to vote, don't you have to inform yourself? It's part of living in a democracy.

BRADT: What about the romantic notion of the artist as someone who lives in an ivory tower and is apolitical, concerned only with his or her small slice of the artistic world?

KENYON: There are as many different kinds of poets as there are engineers or dentists. I'm trying to think if I know any poets who are not political. I can't think of a single poet who is not inclined to get into demonstrations, sign petitions. How can you be a reasonably intelligent person and not, in this time and place, be involved? You can't. The alternative is absolute despair.

BRADT: In your "Proposal" you urge your fellow writers to give public readings and performances. Why is it important to make the arts public? How important is it that your work, say, gets to the public?

KENYON: I want it to get to the public. Art isn't a luxury for the privileged few, and it isn't just private. It may begin in solitude, but it is communication with the reader or the listener. It *does* matter that my work be published, made public, go out into the world, and work whatever effect it has. After the "Proposal" was in the newsletter, everybody called *me* and asked me to do a reading, so I was traipsing all over the place for months after that, doing readings for nothing as I had advocated in the article.

Every year I do a certain number of things for free. I just did an afternoon workshop for the Sullivan County teachers of adult literacy. I go into schools; I think it's important that artists get into the schools and other places where they will encounter people who have never heard a poetry reading, who have no occasion otherwise to encounter a writer. Lots of people think that the good writers are all dead!

BRADT: We assume that poetry matters. Why does it matter?

KENYON: It matters because it's beautiful. It matters because it tells the truth, the human truth about the complexity of life. As Akhmatova says, "It is joy and it is pain." It tells the entire truth about what it is to be alive, about the way of the world, about life and death. Art embodies that complexity and makes it more understandable, less frightening, less bewildering. It matters because it is consolation in times of trouble. Even when a poem addresses a painful subject, it still manages to be consoling, somehow, if it's a good poem. Poetry has an unearthly ability to turn suffering into beauty. When Don was recuperating I had Elizabeth Bishop's poems with me, and I would disappear into that book for minutes at a time, go into that world, and it was a safe place, and a very interesting place. Someone with a marvelous mind and spirit inhabits those poems.

BRADT: You've been called a contemplative poet and compared to Emily Dickinson. How do you respond to those comments?

KENYON: To be mentioned in the same breath with Emily Dickinson makes my day. If by contemplative you mean one who mediates on religious matters, I guess we both do that in our work. Dickinson thinks a lot about her soul, and I think a lot about mine. She thinks about her relation to God—a God who is distant, and rather cruelly arbitrary. In many of my poems I am searching, clumsily, for God. We are both full of terror, finally, and puzzlement, at the creation.

BRADT: What is the source of your poems? Where do they come from?

KENYON: They come from a number of sources. Finally, I guess I do not exactly know. I would say that poetry comes partly from having had a fair amount of solitude in my childhood. I grew up in the country outside Ann Arbor, Michigan. We didn't have many neighbors, and the neighbors we had didn't have kids, so I turned inward at a fairly early age. That probably has more to do with my being a poet than almost anything else. That, and the fact that when I was first introduced to poetry, which was not till I was in junior high school, I was terribly drawn by the strong emotions that I could see were the stuff of poetry. It was okay to have strong emotions in poetry. I had a lot of emotions as a child—and still have as an adult—that are pretty frightening to me. I found that poets are not afraid of feeling. That's what poetry is about; that's really the great subject of poetry. Right away I recognized poetry as a safe haven.

So where do poems come from? Primarily, I think, from childhood. That's when I fell under the thrall of nature. I spent long hours playing at the stream that ran through my family's property. We lived on a dirt road near the Huron River, across from a working farm. I fell in love with the natural world when I was a kid, so my poems are full of the natural world. I use it again and again as a way of talking about something inward. If you read my poems you would not know you were in the twentieth century, because there are no airplanes or computers or E-mail.

BRADT: At what point in the making of a poem do formal concerns, like lineation, stanzas, come into play?

KENYON: Virtually from the beginning. If I showed you a poem with all of its drafts, you could see for yourself how the language changes, how the poem grows and comes into focus, pulls together. At first it's a kind of blind activity. Things come to me when I'm in a certain frame of mind. I sometimes have the feeling that I'm taking dictation. Words suggest themselves. Sometimes I'm not entirely sure of their meaning myself, so I look them up and find that maybe on some deep level I *did* know what that word means, and it just happens to be the *perfect* word. There's a tremendous sense, when I'm working well, that I'm getting a big boost from somewhere. I couldn't tell you where.

BRADT: May Sarton says that poets are chosen.

KENYON: It's pretty weird. I didn't choose poetry really. It seems to be the only thing I'm fit to do. I could be a landscape gardener if I needed to have a job in some other realm. They're both art, both arranging and rearranging things. Almost always if I search I can find something in the natural world—an objective correlative in Eliot's phrase—that embodies what I'm feeling at the moment. That's when a poem really takes off. For instance, I wrote a poem recently called "Coats," in which I'm going into Dartmouth Hitchcock Hospital and a man is coming out of the hospital with a distraught look on his face, carrying a woman's coat over his arm. I see that, and I know what's happened. That poem threw itself at my feet: "Write me! Write me!" I found that by talking about the coats—the man's coat and the woman's coat—I was able to write the poem. I made up the part about the man's coat in this poem. I say that even though the day was warm, he had zipped his own coat and tied the hood under his chin, "as if preparing for ir-remediable cold." It's only three stanzas long, about twelve lines, and it's all about the coats. Maybe he was taking his wife's coat to the cleaner. I doubt it; the emotional truth for me was that he had lost his wife. Lots of people would walk past that man without seeing his situation. I couldn't help seeing it!

BRADT: Who are the writers you go back to for enjoyment and per-haps for inspiration?

KENYON: I've been most excited about John Keats, Anna Akhma-tova, Elizabeth Bishop, Robert Lowell, Geoffrey Hill, and Anton

Chekhov. I mention Chekhov last, but he really belongs at the head of the list, oddly enough. His compassion, his delicate humor, and his profundity seem to me *most* enviable. And of course his brilliant use of physical detail.

BRADT: How did you become interested in Akhmatova?

KENYON: Fourteen or fifteen years ago, Don's old friend Robert Bly was visiting. As he always does he asked me what I was working on. I showed him some poems that I had been working on, and he read them thoughtfully, then looked up and said, "It's time for you now to take a writer and work with that writer as a master." I wasn't even sure what he meant, but I said, "I can't have a man as a master." He said without missing a beat, "Then read Akhmatova." So I began collecting translations of Akhmatova, and I found, much to my dismay, that I didn't think any of the translations were good. So as a kind of exercise in close reading I began collecting all the versions I could of a given poem, and then attempting to write my own version. That's how the door opened.

After I had been doing this for a while, I wondered if these "versions" had any real accuracy. I met a young woman at a party who was a Russian student at Dartmouth. I told her what I had been doing, and she agreed to read them for me. Lou Teel and I began working together and I began to bring the translations closer and closer to the originals. Then Robert came back for another visit. I showed him my translations and he said, "I want to do a book of these"—for the Eighties Press. So that's how it happened.

BRADT: So you had some help with literal translation?

KENYON: Yes. After Robert told me he wanted to do the book, he said that there was one Russian scholar he wanted me to work with—Vera Sandomirsky Dunham, an émigré and a very literary person who knows all the subtleties of both languages. Both he and Louis Simpson prevailed on Vera to work with me, and then the project really got underway. Over the next five years I made periodic trips to Vera's home on Long Island and we worked together.

In working on the translations I became so close to those poems that I forgot they weren't mine. It was only after I got that close that I could feel a bit of freedom in translation. Translation is a necessary evil, and especially difficult if you are uncomfortable with the notion of compromise.

BRADT: My favorite observation on translation is Willard Trask's. Someone commented to him that translation is impossible, and he said, "Of course. That's why I do it." It takes a lot of nerve.

KENYON: It's a solemn pledge. You want to be as accurate as possible, but sometimes you have to change literal details to tell the emotional truth of the poem. You can get weak knees, and I think you should. Translation is an uncomfortable business. I struggled with Akhmatova, struggled not to change her images in particular. Then I would turn to my own poems with this tremendous sense of freedom, and I began to feel some power in my own work for the first time—I'm sure as a direct result of working with those translations. Now in my own work, I saw that there was nothing to limit me but my own imagination. Robert had told me that if I worked on translations they would repay me ten times over for the effort I put into them, and I thought *Yeah*. But I really got going in my own work after I did these translations. I know that if I had not worked so hard on Akhmatova I would never have experienced that surge of power. It was very exciting, and I wrote most of the poems in *The Boat of Quiet Hours* in the years during and right after I had been working on the translations.

BRADT: To what extent is sound important in translation, do you think?

KENYON: It is important. My translations were free-verse translations of rhymed and metered poems, and a lot of people would get off the bus right there. They would say, "You've already lost a good part of what makes the poem wonderful." That's why I say translation is a necessary evil. Either you sacrifice the sound patterns in order to keep the images intact or you sacrifice the images in order to keep the sound intact.

BRADT: Sometimes you can do both in isolated moments.

KENYON: It's rare when you can. You're going to sacrifice either image, or form and sound, and of the two the one I would be most reluctant to lose is the integrity of the images. The images in a good poem come from a deep place, and they give the poem a sense of cohesion. Almost everything else can be tinkered with, but if that is tinkered with, the whole work flies apart. Again and again I saw translations of these poems that had no respect for their psychic wholeness. The translators might have been fairly clever at their rhymes, but it was word games, not poetry. I came to believe in the absolute value of the image when I was working on these poems by Akhmatova. In one of her poems, talking about parting from a lover with whom she's had a spat, she says, "The glove that belongs on my right hand I put on my left hand." Can't you see this flustered, red-faced, confused, frightened woman with a wild look on her face? It's all there in that image.

BRADT: You've lived here at Eagle Pond for almost twenty years now. Have you become a poet of this place, do you think?

KENYON: Yes, I think so. I didn't really get going in my work until we came here. I have all the time in the world here. I had to do something to fill those hours, so I began to work more. I used to work only when the spirit moved, but when we came here I began to write every day, and that was a very important step for me. Inherent in that decision to work every day was the admission to myself that I was getting serious about this poetry business. It was not like learning to upholster furniture or growing plants under lights. It was something more serious.

Only two poems in all the things I've published were not written here. For one thing, living here gave me a subject. I was getting to know this place for the first time, and poetry depends a lot, I think, on the state of wonderment. Poets renew for us the awe we feel at creation. The things I noticed about this place were all subjects for poems, and I suddenly had a broad view. That was immensely important. This is such a beautiful place. It's still such an amazement that we live here among these mountains and hills. I think if Don and I had stayed in Ann Arbor and he had gone on teaching, our lives would have been very different, much more suburban and academic. Our move here permitted him to do something that he had wanted to do for a long time, to strike out on his own and go freelance, and that's precisely what he did. He was ready to do that but I think it took nudging from me to get him to do what he wanted to do. Moving here has been critical for both of us in our development as artists. This is the vale of soul-making, as Keats says. This place has made us both considerably different people. The sense of community here is something I never experienced in Ann Arbor.

BRADT: Would you describe your work habits as a writer?

KENYON: When things are going well for me, I wake early and I take the dog and go a couple of miles up Ragged Mountain. Then I come back and tidy up a bit and have breakfast and go to my study. I work all morning—on three or four poems at a time, if I'm lucky. I've found that working on one thing until it's done can make it harder to finish because if you get stuck you just have to put it down, whereas if you're working on a number of things, and you get stuck on one, you can put it down and turn to something else. After lunch, if things are really hot, I'll go back upstairs, but if not, I spend the afternoon doing chores. In gardening season I'm outdoors every day all afternoon, from June till September. I find I need that mix of sedentary work combined with something physical in the afternoon because I'm pretty restless. Holding still for a number of hours is difficult. I have the best of all worlds. When Gus and I go up on Ragged Mountain in the morning, hardly a day goes by that I don't think, *How is it that you have the phenomenal luck to live here?*

BRADT: One of your poems speaks about plants as companions. Does your sense of companionship extend equally to animals?

KENYON: Certainly—and increasingly to plants and even *stones* if you want to know the truth. I see all creation as interconnected. But to get back to your question, we've had five cats in our eighteen years here. Gus is our first dog. I never had lived with a dog until Gus. I'm head over heels for this boy. I start every day of my life going for a run with him. He's my spiritual leader. He's entirely forgiving; he's silly; he has a wonderful sense of humor; he's earnest and hard working; he never comes back without a stick—sometimes they're five or six feet long. All the neighbors pass us on the way to work and laugh. He has an ardent nature, never discouraged. Dogs are wonderful Zen masters. He's very good at living in the present. That's an art.

I think it's important that we learn to live in the present, especially if we face health problems. If we don't, we're going to wake up one day and realize the present is all we have, that's all we ever have, and we've failed to be present to the present. We all have a tendency when we're doing one thing to plan the next thing. In Bill Moyers's program on healing and the mind there's an exercise that involves eating one raisin. The natural object is always the adequate symbol. Both Don and I, days later, were still thinking about this yoga teacher eating the raisin with complete attention. When I'm gulping down a sandwich on the run because I have to go someplace or do something, that crazy raisin will come back to me and allow me to slow down. It's become a mnemonic for "slow down." We gulp down so much life, and it's never really ours that way. It reminds me of Christ saying in the gospels, "He who would save his life must lose it."

BRADT: What do you take that to mean?

KENYON: You really have to turn your complete attention to something large, something that makes you forget who you are and where you are and what you have and what you don't have. You have to bring your awareness completely to this new thing.

BRADT: Suppose you were a modern-day Rilke, and let's say a Ms. Kappus wrote you for advice. And suppose she had at least a glimmer of talent. What would you say to her?

KENYON: I'd say that your art comes out of your life, and you have to keep living until you have enough to write about. Be patient if you can. Find friends whose judgment you trust and work with them on everything you do. Read, read, read. Art begets art, and you need to read—not just English poets but poets of other cultures and times and traditions. Don't be discouraged if the world doesn't beat a path to your door. If anyone had told me when I was beginning to write poems with serious intent, in my twenties, that it would be another ten years before I published a book, I would have said, "I just can't take that kind of time. I'm running on a different timetable." I think I've become more patient with the years; I'm learning to take the long view.

BRADT: Suppose Ms. Kappus asked you, "What's the poet's job?"

KENYON: The poet's job is to tell the whole truth and nothing but the truth, in such a beautiful way that people cannot live without it; to put into words those feelings we all have that are so deep, so important, and yet so difficult to name. The poet's job is to find a name for everything; to be a fearless finder of the names of things; to be an advocate for the beauty of language, the subtleties of language. I think it's very serious stuff, art; it's not just decoration. The other job the poet has is to console in the face of the inevitable disintegration of loss and death, all of the tough things we have to face as humans. We have the consolation of beauty, of one soul extending to another soul and saying, "I've been there too." Remember Frost's lovely little poem, about going out to clear the pasture spring? "You come too," he says.

An Interview with Marian Blue (April 1993)

(with Jane Kenyon and Donald Hall)

MARIAN BLUE: The theory of artistic temperament negates the concept of two artists living harmoniously together; yet you two have worked and lived together for twenty-one years. Do either of you perceive in the other, or yourself, an artistic temperament which has required adjustments or pampering?

JANE KENYON: Whatever an artistic temperament might be.

BLUE: Yes. Is there such a thing on a day-to-day basis? Do you have warning signs you watch for in each other?

KENYON: I think we're well aware of what is happening to each other in terms of whether the work is going well and whether the results are very exciting. We're aware of each other's rhythms. I think Don understands me when work is very absorbing and I just want to be absentminded and not very present.

DONALD HALL: We take care not to intrude, as well. It's important to keep a separateness, a privacy, bounds. If Jane is away and I have to go into her study for some reason, I would never read a manuscript on her desk.

KENYON: No, he wouldn't; and I wouldn't either.

HALL: When one of us is in a dry period or depressed about the work, we may discuss it casually. We don't probe; the worst thing in the world would be for me to say, or for Jane to say, "What are you working on?" or "What's it about?" Our privacy is important and we respect each other's.

Also, I hold back from presenting my work, which is another kind of privacy. I work on a poem for a long, long time without showing it to Jane. I may be desperate to show it to her, desperate for that praise, but I know that once I show it to her, it is no longer something that is absolutely private to me. When a poem, any work, is private to me, its spirit and possibilities are limitless. Once I show it to anyone—Jane is always number one—somebody else's spirit, psyche, tone of voice, has entered that poem. There is something mysterious in the way in which I know when it is all right for another mind to come into this poem. This holding back is essential to me, perhaps more for me than others, but too many people rush to show work to their best friends or spouses.

KENYON: It works that way for me, as well.

HALL: It varies with the poem. A week or two ago I showed you three poems which I had been working on for a long time. That was a case where I had been saying to myself, for maybe five weeks, "Well, maybe tomorrow."

KENYON: I have a little bunch in my desk that I've been meaning to show you—

HALL: And at some point, you'll take a deep breath and say, "What the hell, here—"

KENYON: That's it.

HALL: Normally we'll each save up two or three new poems. When I have a bunch, I think, "Maybe I'll show them to Jane tomorrow," and then I see a word I want to change and think, "Well, maybe one more day." Finally I show them to her and she says, "Perkins . . . ," and she tells me something. She never praises them enough, I can say for sure.

KENYON: I will have saved up work, too, then Don says, "This is going to be good."

HALL: Then she says, "Going to be?" There have been times, though not lately, when we get a little testy. We don't fight, but we get very polite. "Well, thank you very much," or "Oh, really? Isn't that funny; I thought that was the best part," or "Yes, thank you, I'll think about that." Each of us will say, "I'll think about this"; then we go off and do exactly what the other has suggested.

KENYON: That is the funny part. Everything in me resists what Don is saying at the moment he's saying it and when I climb the stairs I'm saying, "He's dead wrong, he just doesn't get this." The next day I sit down, look at his suggestions, and think, "Why don't I just type it up that way to see what it looks like?" Sure enough, he's found something.

BLUE: So you both are most comfortable commenting orally rather than through written notes?

KENYON: Yes. We generally sit together with the manuscript and we talk it over—

HALL: "Get a metaphor!"

KENYON: —then we both start throwing out possible substitutions and he'll say one I like and I'll say "Write that down!" and he'll write it in the margin.

HALL: First, we read the other's work alone. I make little notes in the margin, to remind me what to say. I think you do that, too.

KENYON: Yes.

HALL: Or I cross out a line or a word. I'll take out all her particles. She isn't allowed to say "was making." I write in "made." That's one of my tics. Talking over a poem helps; I might discover that it's not really the word she dislikes but the one right after it that makes the problem: it's not "purple" but it's "passion." Even when she makes a suggestion I don't accept, her criticism might point out a problem; or maybe a misunderstanding demonstrates that I didn't make clear what I meant to say. This discovery allows me to re-enter the poem. This time, a new sensibility helps. When I show poems to Jane, I know from experience that they are probably not finished, but I don't know what's wrong with them.

KENYON: I reach the point where I just can't see one more thing to do with a poem. I've poked and poked. Yet I sense that it needs more. Even if I think it is finished, I still want Don to confirm my opinion. We can't either of us finish poems without each other's critical opinion. Once I have Don's ideas, and the ideas of my workshop, then I can complete the work. Finally, of course, I must please myself, taking some suggestions and rejecting others.

BLUE: Do you hold back your emotional reactions to your work, whether good or bad, as well?

KENYON: Sometimes that holding back is a way of keeping the work out of other activities. There are times when I don't mention that I've started new poems. If the poems don't turn out to be anything, then I won't have to take back what I've said.

HALL: I can remember mentioning to Jane that "I started a new poem the other day." That was after two or three days when I thought the work was going to stick. I don't say I started one five minutes ago because I don't know if I did; I just think I did.

BLUE: These sound like established patterns for mature writers who have shared a long-term relationship. Yet when you first met, Jane was a new writer in a new relationship with an established writer. Did that intimidate you, Jane?

KENYON: I wouldn't apply the word *intimidated* to it, and yet I used to work more freely when Don was gone.

HALL: The first couple of years after we married, you wouldn't write anything except when I left for poetry readings, so there was something—I don't know if "intimidated" is the right word—but there was some pressure. But consider this: I was nineteen years older than Jane—and still am—and I had published four or five books. I also work sixteen hours a day, which means I'm a living reproach. Finally Jane just said to hell with that, and did her own work. I have always thought it was brave of Jane to put her head down and keep writing.

KENYON: It didn't seem brave. No.

BLUE: Yet you were a new writer?

KENYON: Well, I was twenty-three years old and hadn't really done anything—

HALL: You were twenty-two when we met.

BLUE: So it was brave to continue; but in the process did you feel as though you were damming up work, Jane?

KENYON: I was never aware of damming up poems. I worked when the spirit moved, at first, which was not often. Certainly I had no patterns to my work at all . . . I had a job at the Early Modern English Project at Michigan, and spent half the day there. We did discuss my work habits, I'm sure. It may be similar to my interest in the piano when I was growing up; I never played when anyone else was in the house. It was difficult to submit poems to editors. It was difficult to publish, and difficult not to publish.

BLUE: How did that type of tension affect your ability to critique each other's work?

HALL: Jane and I were student and teacher and friends for some time before anything romantic happened. When we were first married, we had to cope with that earlier relationship. I couldn't criticize her poems, because then I became the teacher. It was psychically confusing; her husband suddenly turns into Professor Hall. The solution—and this is comic—was that we needed a third person. When Gregory Orr would join us, then I could say anything about Jane's poems and she could say everything about mine. Greg's presence made it a workshop in which we were equals.

KENYON: That was a very felicitous discovery.

HALL: After two and a half years of working with Greg, he went to Virginia and we went to New Hampshire. By then, Jane and I could read each other's work. We didn't need Greg.

BLUE: Did you have the same trouble accepting criticism from Jane as you had giving it, Don?

HALL: I don't recall any difficulty, and it would not be likely. When I taught writing, usually once a year toward the end of the term, I brought in some of my own poems. Then my own standards were hurled back at me! I took advice from students.

When Jane was a student, long before there was anything else, I remember once in office hours when something in one of her poems made me think of a poem of mine; I pulled it out and worked on it right in front of her and asked for her help.

BLUE: Your authority, [Jane], confidence, has grown during the time you and Don have been married. How do you perceive Don's influence on your development as a writer, Jane?

KENYON: You can see for yourself that our poems do not resemble each other at all. But whatever it is that I know about writing poems,

I have learned most of it from being with Don, moving to his ancestral farm, keeping my ears open when his peers came to visit. One very important thing I've learned from Don is to be ambitious. Just do it, and take the knocks and praise as they come.

Of course I've had to establish and learn to honor my own habits of work, my own pace, my own areas of interest and struggles. When we married, he had long since established all of these things for himself. My work habits have evolved over time, just as his had. As part of that, my own group of peers has been equally important to my development of skills and nerve.

BLUE: In the past, Don, you've mentioned that your work on essays was almost play but that poetry was more of a challenge. Does living with a poet make writing poetry more of a challenge?

HALL: No. Earlier, I lived with someone who was not a poet. Sharing the experience allows us to understand each other's challenges. This is all good; not every single thing about two writers under the same roof is good, but I find it a confirmation to live with someone whose endeavors, whose desires, and whose love of art are similar—and who struggles to make that art. This identity of endeavor is comforting. I know I talked about establishing boundaries and being separate, but you only have to establish boundaries when there is something bringing you closely together. That is mildly paradoxical but no real contradiction.

BLUE: What do you think, Jane?

KENYON: I think it is pleasant not to have to explain what I am doing, or trying to do.

BLUE: You've workshopped each other's work a great deal over the past twenty-one years. When you're writing and revising, do you hear the other's voice?

KENYON: Oh, I've internalized Don's little tics. I work with several other friends very closely and I've internalized their tics, too. I just lay these principles on the poem like a grid when I'm working on it and I try to anticipate their difficulties with it. That's very important to my work.

HALL: I do the same thing, of course. I know what Jane is going to say; I may be wrong sometimes, but I think I know. In my mind I hear her voice telling me not to do something and I get mad at her— this is all in my imagination. I know that when I repeat a word, words repeated close to each other, Jane is always going to object; therefore I watch for this habit of mine, which I suppose is faintly Victorian. Sometimes I get the repetition out before she sees the poem. But then if I really like the repetition, and she criticizes it, I am apt to think, "Oh, that's just one of Jane's things." There are typical stylistic aspects to her poems, like the repetitions in mine, that I am apt to object to and that she can therefore dismiss. Not that she always dismisses them. Often when she makes a joke, I don't like the joke, not in the poem. But of course, in spite of my familiarity with her habits and work, still she often astonishes me with some of her moves.

There is a danger in expecting criticism, that you'll censor yourself and not allow yourself to go in certain directions—

KENYON: Yes. I always watch for that.

HALL: It's essential for each of us, for anyone, to have more than one reader. We're each other's first reader but not the last. Jane has in particular two female friends. I do my workshops by mail usually.

KENYON: We need other people to find a balance and to see what we are doing from a variety of perspectives.

HALL: Back to your question about hearing the other's voice, sometimes that shows up in other ways. I had a poem that included the phrase "exhalations of timothy," which was a direct steal from Jane. One day before I showed it to her, I realized I had stolen from her, changed the image, and told her. She said, "Watch your ass."

KENYON: I count on Don and my other friends, Alice Mattison and Joyce Peseroff, to catch me if I'm unintentionally taking something from another poet. I stole something from Geoffrey Hill once without knowing it, and I just felt sick about it.

HALL: I ended an elegy poem with a quote from scripture shortly after you had written a poem that closed with scripture.

KENYON: That didn't seem terribly serious to me.

HALL: It did for a moment!

KENYON: Did it?

HALL: Oh, yes, I remember. You were annoyed.

BLUE: As you've worked your way into these established patterns of writing and living together, has there ever been any sense of competition between you, or a temptation to compare quality of work?

HALL: When a magazine prints one of us and rejects the other, at the same time, that can be uncomfortable. No big deal. We used to have a problem based more upon the differences in our ages. That we are of different generations was a help because we were not head on head in rivalry; I belong to the generation of the late 1920s and Jane of the late 1940s, a twenty-year gap. But when we were first married, and for about ten years thereafter, we sometimes had a problem when others would treat me as the poet and her as the little wife who wrote poetry, and isn't that adorable? Nobody said those words, but that was the tone.

KENYON: That was definitely the tone.

BLUE: Did people expect you to promote Jane's career, Don?

HALL: Oh, that was a terror.

KENYON: We were very scrupulous in our separateness.

HALL: But however scrupulous we were, you'd still worry that people would think I was promoting you. I had to do less for you than I would for another poet. That was difficult for me. Always in the past, when I found a younger poet whom I admired, I tried to push the poet—publications, awards, fellowships—to call other people's attention to the poetry. Of course I am not allowed to push in connection with Jane! Maybe I have not been perfect—certainly in letters and in conversation I have praised her work to other people; but I have tried not to do anything that she would disapprove of. I do a little editing for magazines, and I edit anthologies, but for a long time she would not let me print her.

Now I feel that I can recommend her or praise her work more openly than I could before, because so many other people have praised her, given her prizes and awards.

KENYON: Yes. We're okay now. But there were many years when I really didn't want to be with Don for readings and festivals.

HALL: It is new that we be together at a festival or a reading. I remember when it changed, about a year and a half ago in Michigan. We did separate readings, then a joint question period with MFA students. Jane got more questions than I did; it was then that Jane said maybe we could read together.

KENYON: When we sense malice behind comparisons, I become upset. People can be incredibly rude. Differences in our ages have little to do with this. Often I think people make much more of that difference than we do. I needed a man capable of complexity. I enjoy

Don's human wisdom and I admire it. It would be very rare indeed in someone younger.

BLUE: How do you perceive the differences in your work, your styles?

KENYON: I think our visions are very different. Don has been writing a long time, and he has passed through many shapes and sizes, if you will, for his poems. He is writing large, ambitious, loose-limbed poems these days, poems in which all his wisdom appears. I am working at one thing—the short lyric. It is all I want, at this point: to write short, intense, musical cries of the spirit. I am a miniaturist and he is painting Diego Rivera murals. I'm not being modest when I say that I am a miniaturist . . .there's nothing remotely modest about trying to write short lyrics in the tradition of Sappho, Keats, and Akhmatova.

BLUE: Have you ever collaborated on a work?

KENYON: In one sense we collaborate on everything.

HALL: I think there are words of Jane's in my poems and words of mine in hers, in the way friends help friends. Of Bly and Simpson and Kinnell, I can say the same; but we don't write collaborative poems. I don't want that.

KENYON: I don't either. I think it would make a sort of monstrous poem.

BLUE: Have you each written a poem in response to a very specific incident that allowed you a chance to immediately compare your work?

KENYON: Yes. We each wrote about the Gulf War.

HALL: As it happens, Jane's poem is a lot better than mine. That's not modesty, just a fact. But it's funny: these poems are gross exaggerations of the differences in men's and women's characters. Mine could not have been written by a woman. Hers could not have been written by a man. When we do our ABAB readings, we don't deliberately pair poems up. Yet, just reading at random, not consulting the other, we constantly refer to the same dog, the same countryside, the same weather—in totally different ways.

KENYON: Although we don't pair up poems for readings, I often ask Don what he plans to read. I like to construct a reading that is a "voice answering a voice" in Virginia Woolf's phrase. If I know the poet's work well enough, in the case of reading with someone other than Don, I might well ask beforehand what she or he plans to read. There is an improvisational aspect to reading with others, but also a communal one.

HALL: I never knew you were doing that!

BLUE: I'm intrigued by the gender differences you've mentioned, since I've read reviews of your works that referred to the feminine awareness in Jane's work and the anima/animus aspect of Don's work, particularly regarding *The One Day*. Could you elaborate on that difference?

KENYON: I don't know if it has ever been clearer than in these Gulf War poems that Don is talking about. My poem begins with tearing up an old nightgown just out of the dryer to put in the rag bag. The thought moves from that act to dismemberment, thence the war, and what happens to ordinary people in the street during an air war.

Now, chez nous, I do the laundry, I'm afraid. Only if my husband had married a woman who refused to do the wash under any circumstances would he a) do the wash, and b) have written this poem. He works long hours, very hard, but he does not do the laundry.

His poem about the Gulf War is all public, declamatory, loud, and outward. But I don't know that such critiques are useful really.

WAYNE UDE: Jane, you've most often mentioned female friends who workshop with you. Is that an aspect of gender-specific focus in your work?

KENYON: That's interesting. I hadn't thought of that, but it's true. Don works with some female poets. I don't work with other men except on certain occasions when they happen to be around. Robert Bly was with us in December for a few days; he flew up to be with Don because he had been ill, which I thought was very sweet. While he was there, he looked over very carefully the new book and made a few suggestions. It was wonderful—really wonderful.

BLUE: Certainly both you and Don do write personal material. Are there times when the personal quality in a poem presents problems for discussing each other's work objectively?

KENYON: That happens; it's something we have to nurture. In the new book, I have a poem about one of Don's first surgeries for cancer and I'm ambivalent about it myself. He says he doesn't mind. When you're living with a writer, as you know, you'd better watch your ass because you might turn up someplace that surprises you.

BLUE: Has Don ever returned a poem to you that he couldn't critique because of its personal nature?

KENYON: Not yet. But I did ask him specifically about this surgery poem. I said, "Do you mind? Does this trouble you?" He said, "No, I not only don't mind, I'm proud." Writing about grief does help to resolve it, because one comes to newer and deeper understanding in the process of writing. Of course there are things I refrain from writing about just as there are things I refrain from saying. Only an idiot says everything!

BLUE: On the opposite side, do the daily concerns of a married couple ever intrude into your ability to critique each other's work, or to receive criticism from each other? Might you, for instance, refuse to discuss a new poem until anger over a domestic issue has been resolved?

HALL: No, and one of the reasons is that we practically never have a fight. Therefore, when we do fight, it is terrible. I know that there are times when Jane is distracted, or maybe very depressed, when I would not trouble her with a poem. I think about her feelings or her fatigue or her mood before I show her a poem. Because I tend to hold poems back, perhaps mood or fatigue provides me with an excuse, from time to time, for withholding a poem a bit longer.

KENYON: There really is very little discord between us. Of course if we have argued about something, we both feel disturbed and it may spill over into our work. I have written about the damage of arguing.

BLUE: *From Room to Room* and *Let Evening Come* both seem very meditative, tranquil. *The Boat of Quiet Hours* carries more harsh sounds, more religious overtones. That surprised me since you were in the same tranquil setting, still living in a way that most of us regard as ideal. Were the poems deliberately collected because of that tone or was there a time in New Hampshire when a change occurred?

KENYON: I think probably the poems that you're referring to in *The Boat of Quiet Hours* are poems I wrote during my father's illness or after his death, in the early 1980s. It took me about five years to write that book and we had entered into a decade in which there was just non-stop trouble, big-time trouble. My father's illness and death. My grandmother's. My aunt's. My own health suffered when I was in my thirties: I had cancer; I had some serious, debilitating infection in one ear which knocked out my sense of balance. I was really very ill for a couple of years and even now I stagger; I had some hearing loss with it. We just had a real bad time of it. The theme is continuing in the 1990s with Don's trouble and his mother's troubles. Life just keeps coming at you. I think all that did make for a loss of self, a loss of self-possession, which was probably good for my work. The new book has a great deal of very painful material in it.

BLUE: Is it still tied to nature and landscape?

KENYON: Yes. It just seems to me that those areas present the perfect area of image. Image is important to me, probably THE most important thing.

BLUE: Your arrival in New Hampshire obviously carried a strong significance in your work. Now you've been there almost twenty years, an amount of time when poets often seek change. Do you ever feel that you can use up that landscape, that place?

KENYON: Never. I've put down very deep roots there. I can't conceive of being anywhere else.

BLUE: The sense of landscape is less prevalent in much of your work, Don; in fact, "Old Roses" is a poem I think of as unusual for you. Did Jane have a strong influence on that work?

HALL: I don't recall that she did. Does it seem—?

KENYON: I probably contributed some botanical thing.

HALL: Doubtless I was calling them tulips or seagulls or something.

KENYON: You had them blooming in August.

HALL: Jane keeps me straight on natural terminology.

BLUE: You talk of your love of the landscape, the rural scene, Jane. Were you raised in the country?

KENYON: Yes. I was born in Ann Arbor and lived there until I was twenty-eight when we moved to New Hampshire. I went to a one-room school until I was in fifth grade. At that time, the Ann Arbor township schools were annexed into the city schools, but I continued to live across the road from a working farm. For me the move to New Hampshire was a restoration of something that I love very deeply because Ann Arbor kept creeping outward to the point where the road was paved and the farmer's fields were subdivided and ugly houses were built. The move to New Hampshire was a restoration of a kind of paradise.

BLUE: Almost a coming home?

KENYON: Yes, it was.

HALL: At the same time, Jane was not a farmer's daughter; her father was a musician. Her father and mother made a union of opposites: a sophisticated house and life in a country setting. I think contrast makes energy and the more different things you can subsume, the more interesting your writing.

BLUE: Do you think your poetry would have developed similarly without the move to New Hampshire, Jane?

KENYON: I don't know. It seems to me that the move opened up a whole area of possibilities. Certainly the move was the beginning of my serious work on poetry. I used to work just when I felt like it. When we moved to New Hampshire, I had twenty-four hours a day, seven days a week to structure for myself and I began working more regularly and began to publish in magazines and pull together my first book.

On the other hand, it wasn't easy. I found total freedom daunting. I was making over my world in that move; I was replacing my outer constraints with new, inner ones, establishing new priorities. As I mentioned, I needed time to establish patterns. Now I work every morning; Don's bringing me a cup of coffee in bed is a small but significant kindness that sets the tone for the day. I almost never write in the afternoon unless I have a deadline, or unless I'm really hot. I have a lot of chores and responsibilities to attend to in the afternoon.

BLUE: Would you recommend the full-time writing life to others?

KENYON: The simple art of becoming a full-time writer will not significantly change your work. There are full-time writers who can't push things to their limits—poets who stop when a thing is "good enough." The amount of time has nothing to do with being bold or fearless, telling the whole truth.

VI

A Poem

※

Woman, Why Are You Weeping?

The morning after the crucifixion,
Mary Magdalene came to see the body
of Christ. She found the stone
rolled away from an empty tomb. Two
figures dressed in white asked her,
"Woman, why are you weeping?"

"Because," she replied, "they have
taken away my Lord, and I don't know
where they have laid him."

Returned from long travel, I sit
in the familiar, sun-streaked pew, waiting
for the bread and wine of Holy Communion.
The old comfort does not rise in me, only
apathy and bafflement.
                              India, with her ceaseless
bells and fire; her crows calling stridently
all night; India with her sandalwood
smoke, and graceful gods, many-headed and many-
armed, has taken away the one who blessed
and kept me.
                    The thing is done, as surely
as if my luggage had been stolen from the train.
Men and women with faces as calm as lakes at dusk
have taken away my Lord, and I don't know
where to find him.

What is Brahman? I don't know Brahman.
I don't know *saccidandana,* the bliss
of the absolute and unknowable.
I only know that I have lost the Lord
in whose image I was made.

Whom shall I thank for this pear,
sweet and white? Food *is* God, *Prasadam,*
God's mercy. But who is this God?
The one who is *not this, not that?*

The absurdity of all religious forms
breaks over me, as the absurdity of language
made me feel faint the day I heard friends
giving commands to their neighbor's dog
in Spanish. . . . At first I laughed,
but then I became frightened.

⚬

They have taken away my Lord, a person
whose life I held inside me. I saw him
heal, and teach, and eat among sinners.
I saw him break the sabbath to make a higher
sabbath. I saw him lose his temper.

I knew his anguish when he called, "I thirst!"
and received vinegar to drink. The Bible
does not say it, but I am sure he turned
his head away. Not long after he cried, "My God,
my God, why have you forsaken me?"

I watched him reveal himself risen
to Magdalene with a single word: "Mary!"

It was my habit to speak to him. His goodness
perfumed my life. I loved the Lord, he heard
my cry, and he loved me as his own.

~

A man sleeps on the pavement, on a raffia mat—
the only thing that has not been stolen from him.
This stranger who loves what cannot be understood
has put out my light with his calm face.

Shall the fire answer my fears and vapors?
The fire cares nothing for my illness,
nor does Brahma, the creator, nor Shiva who sees
evil with his terrible third eye; Vishnu,
the protector, does not protect me.

I've brought home the smell of the streets
in the folds of soft, bright cotton garments.
When I iron them the steam brings back
the complex odors that rise from the gutters,
of tuberoses, urine, dust, joss, and death.

~

On a curb in Allahabad the family gathers
under a dusty tree, a few quilts hung
between lightposts and a wattle fence
for privacy. Eleven sit or lie around the fire

while a woman of sixty stirs a huge pot.
Rice cooks in a narrow-necked crock
on the embers. A small dog, with patches of bald,
red skin on his back, lies on the corner
of the piece of canvas that serves as flooring.

Looking at them I lose my place.
I don't know why I was born, or why
I live in a house in New England, or why I am
a visitor with heavy luggage giving lectures
for the State Department. Why am I not
tap-tapping with my fingernail
on the rolled-up window of a white Government car,
a baby in my arms, drugged to look feverish?

⤐

Rajiv did not weep. He did not cover
his face with his hands when we rowed past
the dead body of a newborn nudging the grassy
banks at Benares—close by a snake
rearing up, and a cast-off garland of flowers.

He explained. When a family are too poor
to cremate their dead, they bring the body
here, and slip it into the waters of the Ganges
and Yamuna rivers.
                    Perhaps the child was dead
at birth; perhaps it had the misfortune
to be born a girl. The mother may have walked
two days with her baby's body to this place
where Gandhi's ashes once struck the waves

with a sound like gravel being scuffed
over the edge of a bridge.

"What shall we do about this?" I asked
my God, who even then was leaving me. The reply
was scorching wind, lapping of water, pull
of the black oarsmen on the oars. . . .

Bibliography*

Compiled by Jack Kelleher

Verse

From Room to Room
Cambridge, MA: Alice James Books, 1978
59 p.: ISBN 0914086243 (paper)
CONTENTS: 1. Under a Blue Mountain—'For the Night,' 'Leaving Town,'
'From Room to Room,' 'Here,' 'Two Days Alone,' 'The Cold,' 'This
Morning,' 'The Thimble,' 'Changes,' 'Finding a Long Gray Hair,' 'Hanging
Pictures in Nanny's Room,' 'In Several Colors,' 'The Clothes Pin.' 2. Edges
of the Map—'The Needle,' 'My Mother,' 'Cleaning the Closet,' 'Ironing
Grandmother's Tablecloth,' 'The Box of Beads.' 3. Colors—'At a Motel Near
O'Hare Airport,' 'The First Eight Days of the Beard,' 'Changing Light,'
'The Socks,' 'The Shirt,' 'Starting Therapy,' 'Colors,' 'From the Back Steps,'
'Cages.' 4. Afternoon in the House—'At the Feeder,' 'The Circle on the
Grass,' 'Falling,' 'Afternoon in the House,' 'Full Moon in Winter,' 'After an
Early Frost,' 'Year Day,' 'The Suitor,' 'American Triptych,' 'Now That We
Live.' 5. Six Poems from Anna Akhmatova—'The memory of sun sickens in
my heart . . . ,' 'I know, I know the skis . . . ,' 'Everything promised him to
me . . . ,' 'Like a white stone in a deep well . . . ,' 'Along the hard crest of the
snowdrift . . . ,' 'A land not mine. . . .'

The Boat of Quiet Hours
St. Paul, MN: Graywolf Press, 1986
85 p.: ISBN 0915308878 (paper)
CONTENTS: I. Walking Alone in Late Winter—'Evening at a Country Inn,'

---

*Excerpts from the full bibliography, which is available on our web site:
www.graywolfpress.org

'At the Town Dump,' 'Killing the Plants,' 'The Painters,' 'Back from the City,' 'Deer Season,' 'November Calf,' 'The Beaver Pool in December,' 'Apple Dropping into Deep Early Snow,' 'Drink, Eat, Sleep,' 'Rain in January,' 'Depression in Winter,' 'Bright Sun after Heavy Snow,' 'Ice Storm,' 'Walking Alone in Late Winter.' II. Mud Season—'The Hermit,' 'The Pond at Dusk,' 'High Water,' 'Evening Sun,' 'Summer 1890: Near the Gulf,' 'Photograph of a Child on a Vermont Hillside,' 'What Came to Me,' 'Main Street: Tilton, New Hampshire,' 'Teacher,' 'Frost Flowers,' 'The Sandy Hole,' 'Depression,' 'Sun and Moon,' 'Whirligigs,' 'February: Thinking of Flowers,' 'Portrait of a Figure near Water,' 'Mud Season.' III. The Boat of Quiet Hours—'Thinking of Madame Bovary,' 'April Walk,' 'Philosophy in Warm Weather,' 'No Steps,' 'Wash,' 'Inertia,' 'Camp Evergreen,' 'The Appointment,' 'Sick at Summer's End,' 'Alone for a Week,' 'The Bat,' 'Siesta: Barbados,' 'Trouble with Math in a One-Room Country School,' 'The Little Boat.' IV. Things—'Song,' 'At the Summer Solstice,' 'Coming Home at Twilight in Late Summer,' 'The Visit,' 'Parents' Weekend: Camp Kenwood,' 'Reading Late of the Death of Keats,' 'Inpatient,' 'Campers Leaving: Summer 1981,' 'Travel: After a Death,' 'Yard Sale,' 'Siesta: Hotel Frattina,' 'After Traveling,' 'Twilight: After Haying,' 'Who,' 'Briefly It Enters, and Briefly Speaks,' 'Things.'

Let Evening Come
St. Paul, MN: Graywolf Press, 1990
70 p.: ISBN 155597130X (cloth); ISBN 1555971318 (paper)
CONTENTS: 'Three Songs at the End of Summer,' 'After the Hurricane,' 'After Working Long on One Thing,' 'Waking in January before Dawn,' 'Catching Frogs,' 'In the Grove: The Poet at Ten,' 'The Pear,' 'Christmas Away from Home,' 'Taking Down the Tree,' 'Dark Morning: Snow,' 'Small Early Valentine,' 'After the Dinner Party,' 'Leaving Barbados,' 'The Blue Bowl,' 'The Letter,' 'We Let the Boat Drift,' 'Spring Changes,' 'Insomnia,' 'April Chores,' 'The Clearing,' 'Work,' 'Private Beach,' 'At the Spanish Steps in Rome,' 'Waiting,' 'Staying at Grandma's,' 'Church Fair,' 'A Boy Goes into the World,' 'The Three Susans,' 'Learning in the First Grade,' 'At the Public Market Museum: Charleston, South Carolina,' 'Lines for Akhmatova,' 'Heavy Summer Rain,' 'September Garden Party,' 'While We Were Arguing,' 'Dry Winter,' 'On the Aisle,' 'At the Winter Solstice,' 'The

Guest,' 'Father and Son,' 'Three Crows,' 'Spring Snow,' 'Ice Out,' 'Going
Away,' 'Now Where?,' 'Letter to Alice,' 'After an Illness, Walking the Dog,'
'Wash Day,' 'Geranium,' 'Cultural Exchange,' 'Homesick,' 'Summer: 6:00
A.M.,' 'Walking Notes: Hamden, Connecticut,' 'Last Days,' 'Looking at
Stars,' 'At the Dime Store,' 'Let Evening Come,' 'With the Dog at Sunrise.'

Constance
St. Paul, MN: Graywolf Press, 1993
59 p.: ISBN 1555971954 (cloth); ISBN 1555971962 (paper)
CONTENTS: I. The Progress of a Beating Heart—'August Rain, after
Haying,' 'The Stroller,' 'The Argument,' 'Biscuit,' 'Not Writing,'
'Windfalls.' II. "Tell me how to bear myself . . ."—'Having It Out with
Melancholy,' 'Litter,' 'Chrysanthemums,' 'Climb,' 'Back,' 'Moving the
Frame,' 'Fear of Death Awakens Me.' III. Peonies at Dusk—'Winter
Lambs,' 'Not Here,' 'Coats,' 'In Memory of Jack,' 'Insomnia at the
Solstice,' 'Peonies at Dusk,' 'The Secret.' IV. "Watch Ye, Watch Ye"—
'Three Small Oranges,' 'A Portion of History,' 'Potato,' 'Sleepers in Jaipur,'
'Gettysburg: July 1, 1863,' 'Pharaoh,' 'Otherwise,' 'Notes from the Other
Side.'

Otherwise: New & Selected Poems
St. Paul, MN: Graywolf Press, 1996
230 p.: ISBN 1555972403 (cloth); ISBN 1555972667 (paper, 1997)
NOTE: Afterword by Donald Hall, pp. 217–220; Index
CONTENTS: *New Poems*—'Happiness,' 'Mosaic of the Nativity: Serbia,
Winter 1993,' 'Man Eating,' 'Man Waking,' 'Man Sleeping,' 'Cesarean,'
'Surprise,' 'No,' 'Drawing from the Past,' 'The Call,' 'In the Nursing
Home,' 'How Like the Sound,' 'Eating the Cookies,' 'Spring Evening,'
'Prognosis,' 'Afternoon at MacDowell,' 'Fat,' 'The Way Things Are in
Franklin,' 'Dutch Interiors,' 'Reading Aloud to My Father.' From *From
Room to Room*—'For the Night,' 'From Room to Room,' 'Here,' 'Two Days
Alone,' 'This Morning,' 'The Thimble,' 'Changes,' 'Finding a Long Gray
Hair,' 'Hanging Pictures in Nanny's Room,' 'In Several Colors,' 'The
Clothes Pin,' 'The Needle,' 'My Mother,' 'Cleaning the Closet,' 'Ironing
Grandmother's Tablecloth,' 'The Shirt,' 'From the Back Steps,' 'At the
Feeder,' 'The Circle on the Grass,' 'Falling,' 'Afternoon in the House,' 'Full

Melancholy,' 'Litter,' 'Chrysanthemums,' 'Back,' 'Moving the Frame,' 'Winter Lambs,' 'Not Here,' 'Coats,' 'In Memory of Jack,' 'Insomnia at the Solstice,' 'Peonies at Dusk,' 'Three Small Oranges,' 'Potato,' 'Sleepers in Jaipur,' 'Gettysburg: July 1, 1863,' 'Pharaoh,' 'Otherwise,' 'Notes from the Other Side,' 'The Sick Wife.'

NOTE: The following poems were omitted from this collection—from *From Room to Room*—'Leaving Town,' 'The Cold,' 'The Box of Beads,' 'At a Motel near O'Hare Airport,' 'The First Eight Days of the Beard,' 'Changing Light,' 'The Socks,' 'Starting Therapy,' 'Colors,' 'Cages,' 'After an Early Frost.' From *The Boat of Quiet Hours*—'The Painters,' 'Killing the Plants,' 'Teacher,' 'Whirligigs,' 'April Walk,' 'No Steps.' From *Let Evening Come*—'Waiting,' 'Three Crows,' 'Spring Snow,' 'Cultural Exchange,' 'At the Dime Store.' From *Constance*—'Windfalls,' 'Climb,' 'Fear of Death Awakens Me,' 'The Secret,' 'A Portion of History.'

Uncollected Poems

"What It's Like"
Ploughshares, v. 5, n. 2, 1979, p. 58.

"Indolence in Early Winter"
New Letters, v. 47, n. 1, Fall 1980, p. 23
Reprinted in *New Letters*, v. 49, n. 3/4, Spring/Summer 1983, p. 33.

"At the IGA: Franklin, New Hampshire"
Ontario Review, n. 31, Fall–Winter 1989, p. 87.

Translations

Twenty Poems of Anna Akhmatova
Translated from the Russian by Jane Kenyon with Vera Sandomirsky Dunham
[St. Paul, MN]: Eighties Press/Ally Press, [1985]
53 p.: ISBN 0915408309 (paper)
Introduction by Jane Kenyon, pp. 1–6.

Along the Hard Crest of the Snowdrift (poem) [broadside]
Anna Akhmatova
Translated from the Russian by Jane Kenyon
In *Poetry in Motion: [1992–1996]*. New York, NY: New York City Transit
    Authority / Metropolitan Transportation Authority, [1992–1996]
11 x 28 inches; reprinted with the permission of Donald Hall
Multicolored; printed on glossy card stock; upper border has title and re-
    production of decorations from New York subway stations.
Printed in cooperation with the Poetry Society of America
Poetry in Motion: 100 Poems from the Subways and Buses,
    Ed. Molly Peacock; New York: Norton, 1996.

Editor

Green House
Co-editor, with Joyce Peseroff. Danbury, New Hampshire
6 issues produced: Volume 1, Number 1, Spring 1976; Volume 1, Number 2,
    Winter 1977; Volume 1, Number 3, Summer 1977; Volume 2, Number 1,
    Winter 1978; Volume 2, Number 2, Summer 1978; Volume 3, Number 1,
    Winter 1980
NOTE: Includes poems and reviews by Donald Hall, Kathleen Spivack,
    Ruth Stone, Alice Mattison, Caroline Finkelstein, Jane Kenyon, Joyce
    Peseroff, W. D. Snodgrass, Jean Valentine, Gregory Orr, Robert Bly, and
    others.

Contributor

The Third Coast: Contemporary Michigan Poetry
Ed. Conrad Hilberry et al.
Detroit, MI: Wayne State University Press, 1976
296 p.: ISBN 0814315674 (cloth); ISBN 0814315682 (paper)
NOTE: Jane Kenyon, pp. 118–126; includes photograph, biography, and four
    poems: 'Cages,' 'The Circle on the Grass,' 'The Suitor,' 'At a Motel near
    O'Hare Airport.'

Good Company: Poets at Michigan
Edited and with photographs by Jeanne Rockwell
Ann Arbor, MI: Noon Rock Press, 1977. [xiv], 70 p.: ISBN 096029340X
(paper)
NOTE: Includes the poem, 'From Room to Room,' p. 14, a photograph of
the poet, p. 15, and the poet's biography, p. 62. Also includes sections on
Donald Hall, Joyce Peseroff, Robert Bly, and Bert Hornback.

Three Songs at the End of Summer (poem)
In *The Best American Poetry 1989*, pp. 97–98
Ed. Donald Hall
New York: Scribner's, 1989. 293 p.: ISBN 0684190958 (cloth);
ISBN 0020441827 (paper), Macmillan
NOTE: Also includes biography and Jane Kenyon's commentary on the
poem, p. 266. Poem originally appeared in *Poetry*.

Let Evening Come (poem)
In *The Best American Poetry 1991*, p. 119
Ed. Mark Strand
New York: Scribner's, 1991. 326 p.: ISBN 0684193116 (cloth);
ISBN 0020698445 (paper), Collier Books
NOTE: Also includes biography and Jane Kenyon's commentary on the
poem, p. 292. Poem originally appeared in *Harvard Magazine*.

Walking Swiftly: Writings in Honor of Robert Bly
Ed. Thomas R. Smith
St. Paul, MN: Ally Press, 1992. 287 p.: ISBN 0915408481 (cloth);
ISBN 0060975261 (paper), HarperPerennial, 1993
NOTE: Includes Jane Kenyon's essay *Kicking the Eggs*, pp. 83–85.

Having It Out With Melancholy (poem)
In *The Best American Poetry 1993*, pp. 121–125
Ed. Louise Glück
New York: Macmillan/Collier Books, 1993. 287 p.: ISBN 0020698461
(paper)

NOTE: Also includes biography and Jane Kenyon's commentary on the poem, p. 245. Poem originally appeared in *Poetry*.

Words for a Warrant (poem)
Jane Kenyon and Donald Hall
In *Town of Wilmot, New Hampshire: 1993 Annual Report*
n.l.: n.p., [1994]. Cover Poem: A collaboration by Jane Kenyon and Donald Hall—title page
NOTE: ". . . Jane Kenyon and Donald Hall have collaborated to provide Wilmot and its citizens with a truly unique gift of an original poem which we will treasure for years to come." (p. 6—"Report of the Selectmen").

The Language of Life: A Festival of Poets
Bill Moyers
New York: Doubleday, 1995. 450 p.: ISBN 0385479174 (cloth); ISBN 0385484100 (paper), Main Street Books, 1996
NOTE: This book is based upon the PBS-TV series of the same name and also features an interview with Donald Hall.

Reading Aloud to My Father (poem)
In *The Best American Poetry 1996*, pp. 104–105
Ed. Adrienne Rich
New York: Scribner's, 1996. 318 p.: ISBN 0684814552 (cloth); ISBN 068481451X (paper), Touchstone Books
NOTE: Also includes biography of Jane Kenyon, commentary on the poem by Donald Hall, and an excerpt from the poem 'April, New Hampshire,' by Sharon Olds, pp. 259–260
Poem originally appeared in *Poetry*.

Three Songs at the End of Summer (poem)
In *The Best of the Best American Poetry, 1988–1997*, pp. 163–164
Ed. Harold Bloom
New York: Scribner Poetry, 1998. 383 p.: ISBN 0684842793 (cloth); ISBN 0684847795 (paper)

NOTE: Also includes the poet's biography and Jane Kenyon's commentary on the poem, p. 325. This selection first appeared in *The Best American Poetry 1989*, pp. 97–98.
Poem originally appeared in *Poetry*.

The New Hampshire Writers' Project Sampler:
Ten Years of Literary Performance 1988–1998 [sound recording]
Concord, NH: New Hampshire Writers' Project, 1998
1 compact disk; 71:16
Track 10: Jane Kenyon reads her poems 'Gettysburg: July 1, 1863,' 'Man Eating,' and 'Happiness.' Total time–6:10.
NOTE: Jane Kenyon selections recorded at the University of New Hampshire at Manchester, New Hampshire by Fred Portnoy, Soundworks, Canterbury, NH, 1993. Liner booklet includes biographical notes. The disk also includes two poems by Donald Hall, 'Names of Horses,' and 'Ox Cart Man.'

Broadsides

Full Moon in Winter (poem)
Port Townsend, WA: Copper Canyon Press, 1980
6 x 9.5 inches, an unknown number of copies were signed by the author
NOTE: Included in the 23 broadside *Port Townsend Portfolio 1980*, in an edition of 205 copies, by participants in the 1980 Centrum Poetry Symposium.
Poem is from *From Room to Room* and is included in *Otherwise*.

Man Eating (poem)
Concord, NH: William B. Ewert, 1994[June]. Printed at Firefly Press [Somerville, MA]
6.5 x 10.5 inches. 40 copies printed, signed by the author
NOTE: Poem originally appeared in *The Atlantic Monthly* and is included in *Otherwise*.

Otherwise (poem)

St. Paul, MN: Graywolf Press, 1996

9 x 13 inches

NOTE: Printed in February 1996 by Graywolf Press on the occasion of the
publication of *Otherwise*. Poem originally appeared in *Harvard
Magazine* and is included in *Constance* and *Otherwise*.

Dutch Interiors (poem)

Concord, NH: William B. Ewert, [March]1996. Woodcut, relief engraving
by Barry Moser

7 x 11 inches; 60 copies printed, signed and numbered by Moser

NOTE: Poem originally appeared in *Poetry* and is included in *Otherwise*.

Let Evening Come (poem)

[n.l.: n.p., n.d.]

6 x 9 inches

Produced for a memorial tribute: Remembering Jane Kenyon, at the
Friends Meeting House, Tuesday, 30 April 1996 in New York City, with
readings and reminiscences by Donald Hall, Robert Bly, Galway
Kinnell, Alice Mattison, Marie Howe, and Sharon Olds.

NOTE: Poem originally appeared in *Harvard Magazine* and is included in
Let Evening Come and *Otherwise*.

Reading Aloud to My Father (poem)

[n.l.]: David R. Godine, 1996

6.75 x 11.5 inches.

NOTE: This broadside was printed by the Associates of David R. Godine on
the occasion of The Memorial Tribute to Jane Kenyon held at Emerson
Hall, Harvard University, 3 May 1996. This poem originally appeared in
Poetry and is included in *Otherwise*.

At the Winter Solstice (pocm)

Concord, NH: William B. Ewert, [December] 1996. [Somerville, MA]:
Firefly Press. Woodcut, relief engraving by Barry Moser

8 x 14.75 inches; 75 copies printed, signed by Moser

NOTE: Poem originally appeared in *Let Evening Come,* and is included in
Otherwise.

Photographer

Dock Ellis in the Country of Baseball
Donald Hall with Dock Ellis
New York: Coward, McCann & Geoghegan, 1976. 254 p.:
    ISBN 069810658X (cloth)
NOTE: Thirteen photographs by Jane Kenyon, including front and rear
    book jackets

Video Recordings

Poets Read Their Work, Donald Hall and Jane Kenyon
Stony Brook, NY: Educational Communications Center, State University
    of New York at Stony Brook, 1977
Executive producer, Louis Simpson; director, Richard de Simone
Series: Stony Brook Visiting Poets Series; 6
NOTE: Also issued as audiocassette. Use restricted to Educational
    Communications Center.

The Poetry of Jane Kenyon, Ai, Lawrence Kearney, and Kathleen Spivak
Stony Brook, NY: Poetry Center Production, State University of New York
    at Stony Brook, 1978
Director, Harris Schlessinger; producer, Gerry Podd
Series: British-American Poetry Festival videotapes
NOTE: Also issued as audiocassette. Use restricted to the SUNY at Stony
    Brook Poetry Center.

A Life Together: Donald Hall and Jane Kenyon
Princeton, NJ: Films for the Humanities, Inc., 1994
56 minutes; The Moyers Collection; FFH 4917
First broadcast on PBS, 17 December 1993 as *Bill Moyers' Journal*

Jane Kenyon: A Celebration of Her Life and Works
Recorded 26 October 1995, University of New Hampshire Library,
    Durham, NH

Also available on audiocassette
NOTE: Poets Mekeel McBride, Charles Simic, and Donald Hall read Jane
   Kenyon's verse and relate special remembrances of her life.

Jane Kenyon: A Memorial Tribute
Introduced by Stratis Haviaras and Elise Paschen.
Held 3 May 1996 at Emerson Hall, Harvard University, Cambridge, MA
1 videocassette; 84 minutes
On deposit at the Woodberry Poetry Room, Harvard University,
   Cambridge, MA
NOTE: Includes readings by Donald Hall, Robert Bly, Geoffrey Hill, Joyce
   Peseroff, and Alice Mattison, among others.

Sound Recordings

Poetry and Prose Reading
Jane Kenyon, Frank Bidart, Carolyn Chute, Justin Kaplan; introduced by
   Dewitt Henry and Jennifer Rose
1987; 1 sound cassette; 85 minutes
Located at the Woodberry Poetry Room, Harvard University, Cambridge,
   MA
NOTE: Use restricted to Poetry Room.

Jane Kenyon and Judith Moffett reading their poems
1988: 1 sound tape reel (ca. 60 min.)
NOTES: Recorded 8 March 1988 in the Coolidge Auditorium at the Library
   of Congress in Washington, D.C. Sponsored by the Gertrude Clarke
   Whittall Poetry and Literature Fund, Library of Congress, Washington,
   D.C. Recorded for the Archive of Recorded Poetry and Literature.

Poems to a Listener: Readings and Conversation with
Contemporary Poets
Interviewed by Henry Lyman
Distributed nationally to public radio stations in the United States
30 minutes/interview segment

NOTE: Interviews with Jane Kenyon and readings of her poems recorded at Eagle Pond Farm, 1981, 1984, 1992.

Jane Kenyon: A Memorial Tribute
Introduced by Stratis Haviaras and Elise Paschen
Held 3 May 1996 at Emerson Hall, Harvard University, Cambridge, MA
1 sound tape reel; 84 minutes; mono
Located at the Woodberry Poetry Room, Harvard University, Cambridge, MA
Cassette copy available; DAT cassette copy available
NOTE: Includes readings by Donald Hall, Robert Bly, Geoffrey Hill, Joyce Peseroff, and Alice Mattison, among others.

Scores

Briefly It Enters: A Cycle of Songs from Poems of Jane Kenyon: For Voice and Piano 1994–1996
William Bolcom
[n.l.]: E. B. Marks; Milwaukee, WI: Exclusively distributed by H. Leonard, 1997. 35 p.: ISBN 0793591325 (paper)
Inside cover—"for Benita Valente, soprano, Cynthia Raim, piano, and Donald Hall, in memory of Jane Kenyon"
Includes brief commentary by Donald Hall, p. 2 ("Jane Kenyon's passion for music was as great as her genius for writing poetry....")
NOTE: Poems—'Who,' 'The Clearing,' 'Otherwise,' 'February: Thinking of Flowers,' 'Twilight: After Haying,' 'Man Eating,' 'The Sick Wife,' 'Peonies at Dusk,' 'Briefly It Enters, and Briefly Speaks.'

American Triptych: For Soprano, Flute, Clarinet/Bass Clarinet, Violin, Cello, Piano, and Percussion: On Three Poems by Jane Kenyon
J. Mark Scearce
[n.l.: n.p.], August 1997. [2] p.: paper
NOTE: Includes the poems 'At the Store,' 'Down the Road,' 'Let Evening Come,' p. [2].

Additional Work by / about Jane Kenyon

Bolcom, William. *Let Evening Come: A Cantata*
Text: poems by Jane Kenyon, Emily Dickinson, and Maya Angelou
Premiere—New York City, 1994
Soprano, Benita Valente; piano, Cynthia Raim.

Farrow, Anne. "Into Light All Things Must Fall." *Northeast: The Hartford* [CT] *Courant Sunday Magazine.* 27 August 1995, p. 9.

Hall, Donald. "Life After Jane: An Essay." *Northeast: The Hartford* [CT] *Courant Sunday Magazine.* 27 August 1995, (cover) pp. 6–8.

Blue, Marian. "A Conversation with Poets Donald Hall & Jane Kenyon" In *AWP Chronicle*, May/Summer 1995, Volume 27, Number 6 (cover), pp. 1–8.

Bradt, David. Jane Kenyon Interview. *The Plum Review*, #10, September 1996, pp. 115–128
Interview conducted at Eagle Pond Farm, Wilmot, NH, March 1993.

Bolcom, William. *Briefly It Enters: A Song Cycle*
Sets nine Jane Kenyon poems to music. World premiere, University of Michigan, Ann Arbor, 27 September 1996. Soprano, Benita Valente; piano, Cynthia Raim
Commissioned by Benita Valente
Also performed at the University of New Hampshire, Durham, NH, Herbst Auditorium, San Francisco, CA, The Hopkins Center, Dartmouth, NH, Wisconsin Union Theater, University of Wisconsin, Madison, WI, and the Tisch Center for the Arts, New York, NY
NOTE: The Madison, WI performance was recorded for a Spring 1997 airing on National Public Radio.
For poems, see entry in Scores section.

Germain, Edward. "Jane Kenyon." *Contemporary Poets.* Sixth edition
Ed. Thomas Riggs
New York: St. James Press, 1996
Essay on Jane Kenyon; with biography, bibliography, pp. 576–578.

"Special Section Dedicated to the Memory of Jane Kenyon." *Xylem: the
University of Michigan Undergraduate Literary Journal.* Volume XII,
Winter 1996, pp. 54–64
NOTE: Includes Laurence Goldstein's essay *Remembering Jane Kenyon,*
pp. 55–58 and Jane Kenyon's poems, 'The Call,' 'Afternoon at
MacDowell,' 'Dutch Interiors,' pp. 59–62.

Life at Eagle Pond: The Poetry of Jane Kenyon and Donald Hall
Internet website—
http://wwwsc.library.unh.edu/specoll/exhibits/kenhall.htm.
Online exhibit created and maintained, 1996, by William E. Ross, Special
Collections Librarian, University of New Hampshire, Durham, NH.

"A Tribute to Jane Kenyon 1947–1995." *Columbia: A Journal of Literature
and Art.* Issue 26, 1996, pp. 154–181
CONTENTS:
Jean Valentine's poem, 'Elegy for Jane Kenyon,' p. 157
Donald Hall's untitled essay on Jane Kenyon, pp. 158–159
Donald Hall, excerpt from his book, *The One Day* (1988), p. 160
Jane Kenyon's poems, 'Alone for a Week,' 'The Suitor,' 'Winter Lambs,'
'Chrysanthemums,' 'Pharaoh,' pp. 161–167, 'Prognosis,' p. 170, and
'Let Evening Come,' p. 181
Donald Hall's poems, 'A Beard for a Blue Pantry,' pp. 168–169, and 'Old
Roses,' p. 180
Maxine Kumin's poem, 'After the Poetry Reading' (inspired by Marie Howe
and in memory of Jane Kenyon), p. 171
Charles Simic's essay, *Jane Kenyon,* pp. 172–173
Sharon Olds's poems, 'To Jane in the Church (to Jane Kenyon, 1947–1995),'
and 'Love (for Donald Hall),' pp. 174–177

Galway Kinnell's poem, 'How Could You Not (for Jane Kenyon, 1947–1995),' pp. 178–179.

Bly, Robert. "The Yellow Dot." Poem from *The Morning Poems* New York: HarperCollins, 1997.

The First Jane Kenyon Conference: 16–18 April 1998 [sound recording] Louisville, KY: Bellarmine College, 1998. 4 audiocassettes: approx. 90 minutes each.

NOTE: Conference featured readings, commentaries and remembrances of Jane Kenyon by Wendell Berry, Galway Kinnell, Alice Mattison, Joyce Peseroff, Gregory Orr, and Donald Hall.

How Could She Not: for Jane Kenyon (1947–1995) (poem) / Galway Kinnell; woodcuts, Ilse Schreiber-Noll
[n.l.]: [I. Schreiber-Noll], © 1998
8.5 x 11 inches. [12]p.

Forthcoming *(Spring, 2000)*

Proceedings of the First Jane Kenyon Conference: 16–18 April 1998 (Cambridge, MA: Peter Lang Press)

JANE KENYON was born in Ann Arbor and graduated from the University of Michigan. She is the author of five collections of poetry: *From Room to Room* (Alice James Books), *The Boat of Quiet Hours* (Graywolf Press), *Let Evening Come* (Graywolf Press), *Constance* (Graywolf Press), and *Otherwise: New & Selected Poems* (Graywolf Press); and translator of *Twenty Poems of Anna Akhmatova* (Eighties Press/Ally Press). Her poems have appeared in many magazines, including the *New Yorker, Paris Review,* the *New Republic,* the *Atlantic Monthly,* and *Poetry.* She lived and worked with her husband Donald Hall in Wilmot, New Hampshire, until her death in 1995.

The text of this book has been set in Adobe Garamond,
drawn by Robert Slimbach and based on type cut by
Claude Garamond in the sixteenth century.
This book was designed by Wendy Holdman,
set by Stanton Publication Services, Inc., and manufactured by
Maple-Vail Book Manufacturing on acid-free paper.

Graywolf Press is dedicated to the creation and promotion
of thoughtful and imaginative contemporary literature essential
to a vital and diverse culture. For further information, visit us
online at: **www.graywolfpress.org**

Other Graywolf titles you might enjoy are:

The Way It Is: New & Selected Poems
WILLIAM STAFFORD

Relations: New & Selected Poems
EAMON GRENNAN

Things and Flesh
LINDA GREGG

Moon Crossing Bridge
TESS GALLAGHER

The Owl in the Mask of the Dreamer: Collected Poems
JOHN HAINES

Feeling as a Foreign Language: The Good Strangeness of Poetry
ALICE FULTON

The Graywolf Silver Anthology